VOLUME 3

LIFE REVISIONS

FALL 2013

EDITED BY

Nina Rubinstein Alonso

Constellations
A Journal of Poetry and Fiction

ISSN 2164-3830

Volume 3 (Fall 2013): Life Revisions

Publisher and Editor
Nina Rubinstein Alonso

Technical Consultant
Jack Miller

Constellations is published annually by Nina Rubinstein Alonso. For submission guidelines, subscriptions, or to contact us for any other reason, please visit our web site at www.constellations-lit.com.

ISBN-13: 978-1494426774
ISBN-10: 1494426773

Cover Image Credit: NASA / Goddard Space Flight Center / Solar Dynamics Observatory.

Table of Contents

Editor's Note

When I settled on the theme "Life Revisions" for this issue, I was thinking of the bumps and shifts of growth, the winding river's hidden rocks and waterfalls, the arid spells, the psychological collisions, the surprises and disappointments, the collapse of relationships—that sort of thing.

The marathon bombing on Boylston Street struck innocents on a fine April day, terrorism in Boston, gun battles in Watertown, much of it close to where we live. Days on lockdown left us numb, hospitals full of people whose lives were taken or devastated. One of the young terrorists used to go to a local high school with kids who considered him a "nice" guy, lacking clues to make anyone think otherwise. The week before this event I strolled down that exact segment of Boylston Street to attend a poetry festival at the Boston Public Library with writers in this issue: Kathleen Spivack, Harris Gardner, Jennifer Jean, Doug Holder, and others. It was a cool day and Boylston Street was hosting a Greek Festival parade.

Writers go on writing as that's what we need to do, though after such shock some of us are silenced, flattened. This is a fractured world where the jolted and wounded self tries to locate what survives, hold dear ones close, search out what's beautiful and civil in a brutal landscape. Surveying this third issue of *Constellations*, the echoes are there. Consider Luke Salisbury's story "Ilona," about a Holocaust survivor who doesn't like the word Holocaust, then Logan Seidl's poem "What America is Doing to Baseball," anticipating our intense response to the World Series win. (His first line starts: "Yesterday I won the world series...") It's about the passion for playing games, the drive to win, which, inverted, is destructive.

Change can be the hardest thing, something we resist, but seek in alternating moods and moments. Helen Silverstein's story "Burn Pile" is about being stuck, unable to get out of a situation or feel "right" staying in it. In Peggy Aylsworth's poem, "How it Was, 1935," the depression crash hits, leaving the formerly well-off in a "fifth floor walk-up," breathing an atmosphere so negative, "I never/heard them laugh out loud."

I'm grateful that the Constellations community is increasing, as we need all our voices. Let this sort of music grow, lest we be deafened by the noises of senseless argument, irrationality, chaos.

Nina Rubinstein Alonso, November 2013

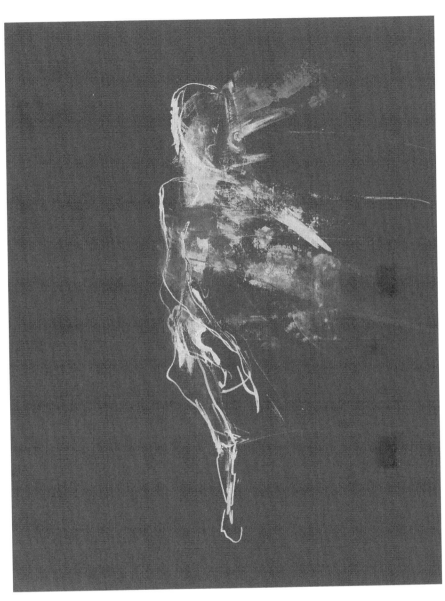

IVAN DE MONBRISON

A Human Figure Translated

Negative photography of an original drawing; ink and acrylic on paper for the original work. (Paris, 2012)

DOUG HOLDER

A Vacant Stare at the Sky

On the phone
my sister-in-law
her voice brittle and cracked
"Oh my God, a bomb at the marathon!"

At the radio
the Towers collapsed for me again
now—
the damning knapsack
...the white smoke
lower extremities
shrapnel
the reporters' constant replay
and I am fixated
worried about my own sorry ass
and then something clutched my throat
as my friends' and family's faces
a cinema of wide-eyed fear
flashed before me
wondering
if they were
at the finishing line.
was it their time?
and when was
mine?

In the aftermath
that woman's vacant stare
at the sky
as if the heavens could answer

"Why?"

HARRIS GARDNER

Notes: Boston, April 17, 2013

My courtship wasn't slow. I moved to Boston in 1980. My first apartment was a one-bedroom, third-floor walk-up at 86 Commonwealth Avenue at the corner of Clarendon Street; then I moved around the corner to a basement one-bedroom apartment on Clarendon Street. I completed the horse shoe when I moved to a one-bedroom at 92 Beacon Street for five years. Then, I moved to the West End in 1990. I lived and worked in Boston for over thirty years.

I always found Boston to be a congenial city offering its bookstores, the MFA and Gardner Museums; Thai Food on Charles Street; the Harvard Gardens on Cambridge Street; The Public Gardens and Boston Common; the rare symphony; the North End and shopping at the Haymarket. I would be remiss if I didn't mention Filene's Basement. (Ferragamo shoes for $48.00, normally $200.00).

Boston has been described as a city of neighborhoods. One thing that they share in common is community. Community is sometimes a fragile thread; however, they have weathered various crises and have become stronger because of them. The Marathon bombs dealt Boston, and perhaps the country, a major, but not fatal, wound to our psyches. Bostonians, New Englanders, and we, as Americans, are resilient people. When confronted by crises, and even in the face of Terror, our resolve only gets stronger. We recovered from 9/11 even though we were changed by it forever. Yesterday's wounds will also heal, eventually.

In times of trauma, a lot of us put aside our differences and forge stronger bonds with our neighbors and as a people. Yes, there is evil; however, we must not lose sight that there is a lot of good to counteract sick sociopaths and other forms of hatred. Healing will begin when the perpetrators of the Marathon Mayhem are caught and face maximum justice. Meanwhile, it is good to continue the processing with poetry, and other thoughts which also have a salutary effect.

Thank you Doug, Tim, Zvi, Rene, and everyone who has helped me deal with and comprehend my own feelings regarding this great tragedy.

Ilona

I stayed late Sunday night after the Bible group to speak to Ilona. It was after eleven, and I had to get up early the next day, but I had something I wanted to say. It was something I never told anyone and I wanted to tell Ilona because Ilona sees things more clearly than anyone I've ever met. She sees pretense and vanity too. I don't think she ever had a banal conversation in her life. Not since the war anyway.

Ilona Karmel is a Holocaust survivor living in Belmont, Massachusetts. She doesn't like the term "Holocaust," and refers to that time as "the war." The day she was liberated, a German in a truck ran her over, killed her mother, and sliced off Ilona's left leg at the knee. She told me she lay there thinking it looked like "a piece of chicken." She doesn't think much of self-pity.

Ilona is a short woman, slightly hunched in the shoulders, with iron gray hair, and remarkable, truly remarkable, pale eyes behind thick glasses—I sometimes think the glasses are to protect the world from her eyes—and very strong forearms and hands. She speaks with a heavy Polish accent but her English is excruciatingly exact. Ilona spent three years in Sweden in various hospitals, undergoing various operations. She sums up those years saying, "Look, they've wheeled out the piece of meat again." Ilona is my mother's age, though their lives were, to say the least, different. Ilona is one of three people I've really wanted to like me. She never had children.

Her house is always clean. We were in the living room. The group, which Ilona says is "the most secular Bible group since the Creation," was reading Dante, which she likes, being neither irritated nor distracted by its Christianity. She sat on the couch with her crutches beside her. I move the other couch back to the ficus tree at the end of the room. The room is back to normal. Opposite the couch, over the fireplace, is a lithograph of the Krakow Cathedral, a blurry pastel of evergreen trees, and a sketch of a fat baby. Ilona watches me, and says, "Dante knows something we know and he knows something we don't know." I turn that over in my mind. I'm talking to someone who knows more than I know and so much I don't.

"I saw *Schindler's List*," I say, sitting down in a chair opposite her. This isn't what I stayed to say, but I like to talk about the war. "Isn't it like Hollywood to make a movie about the war and have a German be the hero?"

Ilona looks at me and says, "You're wrong. The fact one of them did what he did is such a rebuke to the rest. Schindler was a remarkable man. He was in danger twenty-four hours a day. He could have been arrested at any time. No one knows why Schindler did what he did. He saved two of my aunts. He would come to Israel every year and they would do anything for him. No. He was remarkable."

I feel stupid, and out of my depth, which happens with Ilona, but I'd rather be stupid than silent. Sensing my discomfort Ilona says, "That new book, *Hitler's Willing Executioners*. The author was on Chris's show and it made my blood boil." She is talking about Christopher Lydon, a member of the group, who hosts a radio talk show. She pronounces Chris with a long i sound. Chriiis. "A book like that is to make Americans feel smug about themselves." Ilona sits up and looks at me with those eyes that have seen things I can't imagine. "How do you know what you would have done, if your life depended on it? The life of your family? How does anyone know? It was death to help the Jews. A few Poles helped us. Some helped the Germans. Most did nothing. How does anyone know what he would do in that situation?"

"I'm not brave," I say.

"You don't know."

I shrug.

"If the professor really cared about the Holocaust, he'd sell his house in Newton or wherever he lives, and give the money to people in Roxbury. But he's not going to do that, is he?"

Only one lamp was lit—a floor lamp with square shade that illuminates the ceiling and creates a cave-like privacy. Ilona's living room is for talking, not watching television. I eat the last piece of lemon poppy seed cake. "One always baked a cake for guests in Poland," she says. I've never been to her house and not eaten cake.

"I want to tell you something," I say.

Ilona watches me. She has harsh features but her eyes, even behind glasses, and the deep lines in her brow and by her mouth, give her face a generous but stern warmth.

"It happened when Carol and I were separated. You and I had just met."

"I remember," Ilona says. "You used to come here and not say anything."

I tell her about a day when Carol and I were separated and I took our six-year old son Harry canoeing on the Concord River. "It was the first time I ever done anything alone with him."

Ilona nods. She likes Harry. Ilona has a cat, the fattest cat I've ever seen, which Harry calls the "barrel-cat."

I tell her it was a day everything went wrong. I got lost driving there. We went down the river with the wind and couldn't get back until the wind died down. "Every little thing, every chance to be a dad, to be competent, went wrong."

Ilona watches me. The barrel-cat laboriously climbs in her lap and begins to purr.

I tell her how hard Harry tried to paddle, how awful and impotent I felt. But that wasn't what I wanted to tell. What I want to tell was after the river. After we got back and had ice cream at

Friendly's, Harry and I went in the old graveyard in Concord Center, not Sleepy Hollow, the big cemetery where Emerson and the famous writers are buried, but the small ancient-looking one across from the Unitarian church.

"Harry got sad because he saw children's graves and he asked me what happens when you die. I didn't know what to say, so I told him Jesus would take care of him. I'm not a believer but I said it. I said He loved children more than grown-ups, because He said suffer the little children to come unto me when the disciples tried to keep the children quiet."

"You stayed to tell me about your temporary conversion?" says Ilona.

"No," I say. "We crossed Main Street and walked on the green of the Unitarian Church. That wide-pillared, classic New England church. As we walked, my grandmother was beside us. She turned to me. She was smiling. Her face had all the warmth and understanding in the world. It didn't last a second but she was there. She'd been dead for thirty years. But she was beside us. She saw Harry."

"She's the one you loved so much?" says Ilona.

"I don't believe in ghosts. I don't believe in Jesus. But, by the Unitarian church. It was Nanny, who had the love my parents lost or never had. The love Carol and I lost, but got back. It was religious, but that's not the right way to describe it. I don't know how to describe it. What's strange is at the time, it seemed perfectly natural. Not scary. I decided not to tell anyone. If I told Carol, even now, she'd hum the theme from *The Twilight Zone*.

"I didn't tell anyone. A week later, my mother called, and said, 'Have you seen Nanny?' I said, 'What?' and she said, 'I've been praying to her to come to you.' 'What?' I said. 'What?'

"Nothing like that ever happened to me before or since."

Ilona shifts her weight from one side of the couch to the other. She has been watching me carefully. The barrel-cat purrs. "My mother came to me once in a dream. It was by a black river that separated Camp A and Camp B. One was a work camp, the other a death camp. It was more than a dream, but I don't know."

"I don't know either," I say.

"It's a gift," Ilona says. "That's all."

"All right," I say. "A gift."

"It's fine as long as you don't use it to feel good about yourself."

VALENTINA CANO

A Death

You answered me with that last look,
a veil of distance already between us.
I was bleeding out of this world,
skin becoming air,
my voice nothing more than the water's whisper.
What could I do with the seconds
and minutes and hours and days all around me?
Just close my eyes
and feel them pressing,
a wall forever closing in.

The Chase

The man appeared again
as I stumbled through
the glass tunnel of my dreams.
He said nothing,
his arms stretched out,
unmoving bars swaddled in skin.
Even then, I knew to run;
even as shards of memories
leapt out of the walls
and nestled in my skin.
I ran.
I always run.

MARK J. MITCHELL

The Second Plague

She often dreamed of frogs. She didn't know
Why—too much Russian music—one of those
Childhood triggers—loaded, tough to dislodge
As popcorn kernels or a dull boyfriend.
When she noticed it, she wanted it to end,
That's all. It's only abandoned luggage.
Then came that morning when a sunrise croaked
At her and she ribbeted back. A float
Of fear slid down her cheek. She didn't cry.
She rose, calm as a dandelion, cool
And soft. All her frog dreams were slightly blue—
Sad and dirty. Night let this one slip by.
She closed her confused mouth and wrapped knowledge
Around each sound. She knew just how to nudge
The residue dreams left. It wouldn't show
In daylight. Her tongue might snap at a fly,
Her feet might jump a little. An awkward stride
Could mask that. She'd speak in pale quarter notes,
Ignore questions. It worked in her college
Captivity. She was sure she could dodge
Daylight for a while. She'd learn to defend
Memories and mutations. She'd deny
Biology. She'd find a way to hide
In the open. There was no one to fool.

Done Driving

Good Friday. Driving westward with the sun,
Your visor's not quite blocking out low glare,
So you're not quite blind. Red spheres rise between
You and traffic. Fighting the light, your foot's
Too heavy and this car's too fast. The wheel's
Hot, slippery in your hands. It's just a drive
And west was just a whim. Now it's a fight
And you don't know why. Somehow there's a poem
You've forgotten gnawing at your memory—
It seemed urgent in that honors class—
That art. That craft. The new teacher coached you
On meter and rhyme. Those lines, put to page
Four hundred years ago weren't only words,
They were the sort of prayer we can't utter
These days. You slow. Red tail lights bloom ahead.
Cars herd together. Holiday traffic—
Stray daughters, nephews, parents are drawn back—
Falcons to a lure—because of some page
On their calendar whose meaning's misplaced.
And you're driving westward towards the sun,
Alone, worrying a poem you forgot
When you closed that book. And you're almost blind.

Etruscan Book Study

If this theory of thunder is correct
Then you need to stake out
That quadrant of sky where
White birds vanish towards dawn.
We can't waste this night.

And you—yes, you—it's important
That horses remain silent.
See to it. The rest of you
Scatter to the wind and drift
Like petals on running water.

Be sure to leave all your clothes behind.
Now go—all of you—Go!

Timepiece

Spotting a clock in the mirror
She feels her skin start its slow itch.
No sounds—modern clocks will not tick—
But seconds still fall. Her eyes hear
Time, that's her curse. Running her hand
Along her arm, she shivers, breathes
Out without thought. Today she needs
A way out. She will drop like sand
Through the narrow waist an hourglass
Offers—no more numbers for her.
She checks her hair for her escape.
A door below that broken plate
Will open. The mocking mirror
Knows her voice. She knows she can pass.

Ballads
(While listening to John Coltrane at work)

The dead man's sax
Warms up this cool night.
Outside, people walk in moonlight
Under streetlights, trading stories
Of failed trades and bad luck.
Hard shoes sound a hollow backbeat.
The store is empty, bottles aligned
Perfectly, free of dust.
Johnny Hodges starts to croon
"My one and only love…"
And I remember to worry
About you, my trembling girl.
At home. Alone in the dark.
Lamenting what cannot be named.

JOSEPH GIORDANO

Out of Gas

After three *caipirinhas*, Michael didn't notice the difference between C, *cheio* - full and V, *vazio* - empty on the gas gauge, and the '80s pale blue Malibu he'd been given to drive sputtered out along the side of Rua Cezar Moranza on his way back to the Bandeirantes Hotel in Campinas. He'd flown in from New York on Friday, and spent most of Saturday sitting on the bed, eating hearts of palm and *patatas fritas* from room service, while channel-surfing between dubbed Portuguese movies and Brazilian football. The lime, *cachaça* rum, and sugar caipirinhas hit him like a sledge. He poured bubble bath into the Jacuzzi, and when the tub buried him in an avalanche of foam, he decided that the strikingly blue, sunlit sky he saw outside his window demanded he explore.

His new boss, Sergio Almeida, had to fly to Rio de Janeiro the evening Michael arrived. Before he left, Sergio warned him not to walk off the hotel grounds. Guests who'd taken jogs around the motel had been robbed for their running shoes. Sergio said, "Better you not go out, but if you do, go only during the day and take the car. Roll through red lights," he warned. "If you stop, someone may come up to the car with a gun."

Michael checked the new sports-watch he'd bought with the bonus he was given for moving to Brazil. It was about an hour before dark. He stepped out of the car and looked around. Gradations of green flora flooded a rolling landscape of iron-red farmland dotted with blazing red and white bougainvilleas. But there wasn't a building in sight. He took out his white handkerchief and tied it on the car aerial. Maybe someone will stop, he hoped. But after fifteen minutes, not a single car had passed. He wondered if Brazil even had road service. Great, he thought, I don't have a phone and if I did, the only person I could call is Sergio. I'd need to ask him to have one of my new co-workers help the hotshot just arrived from the States. Yeah, the engineer genius we needed to import rather than promote a Brazilian to his position. Drop everything you're doing on a Saturday evening, and rescue the dumb fuck who's run out of gas. Michael thought, no way this is going to end well. Sergio will learn of this incident, and when he does, he'll put me on the next plane to New York with a recommendation that headquarters fire my ass. Michael watched the sun drop in the sky, and he swallowed hard. He thought, I'm in the middle of nowhere, without a clue how to get help, and my wish is that I could make a career-ending phone call.

The image of his mother's face with her "I told you so" look popped into his head. He recalled their last conversation. "Why do you need to move so far? We'll never see you. You can't get a job in New York?"

Michael's mouth dropped when his father spoke up. "Mildred, stop trying to control the boy. He has ambition. If I acted on mine, we wouldn't be forced to skimp on everything."

Michael said, "Mom, you can visit. I'll pay for both air tickets. A tropical climate would be a great place for a getaway."

"I don't need a vacation, and it's too hot for me. Your father gets terrible sunburn. We couldn't possibly come."

"I'll come to New York for Christmas."

"Let's hope we're still alive."

Michael's father pulled him aside. "She'll get over it."

But Michael knew that when it came to reading his mother, his father was always wrong. His mom sent him off with a hug and a face reserved for the bereaved at a funeral.

Brazil was to be his big move. Now, he'd return to New York in disgrace. Michael shook his head.

A beat up, gray Volkswagen Beetle that Brazilians call a Fusca pulled off the highway with headlights off and stopped in front of his car. Two twenty-year-old guys threw open the doors and jumped out.

In the growing darkness they looked like a macumba Mutt and Jeff. One of them carried a revolver. At the sight of the gun, Michael's stomach soured, and coldness gripped his chest. The men both had slicked down black hair and wore tattered, dark shorts and flip-flops. The tall dude with the gun had a toothy grin like a predator. He had on a stained Brahma Chopp tee shirt. His short homie was missing most of his teeth and wore a blue fishnet tank top. Michael raised his hands. His focus narrowed to the pointed pistol and the black cavern inside the barrel that looked like the mouth of the Lincoln Tunnel.

The short guy said something to Michael in Portuguese. When Michael didn't respond, the toothless mouth sliced into an angry sneer. He moved closer to Michael and yelled. He smelled like a sweated jock strap. The guy with the gun spoke, and the short dude realized Michael didn't understand. Toothless put his hands on hips and looked Michael up and down. He pointed to the watch and grunted. Michael handed it over. The watch slipped down the man's forearm, and he brandished it at Michael like it was a head on a pike. He backed Michael up against the car and rifled through his pockets and came up with his wallet and car and motel keys. Toothless pocketed everything, and made motions that Michael should strip off his clothes. Michael stiffened, and his eyes darted between his captors. Tall dude raised the pistol to Michael's face, took a step closer and said, "*Vamanos.*" Michael quickly pulled off his shirt, took off his Nikes and gym socks, unbuckled his khaki shorts and dropped them to his feet. Michael stood naked but for his white briefs and a gold chain around his neck, a present from his mother with a bas-relief medal depicting the Virgin Mary, and an inscription on the back, "To my son on his First Communion." The short dude grabbed at the chain. Michael flinched away and held the piece in his fist. The gunman cocked his pistol. Michael swallowed, slipped the chain over his head, and gave it to toothless.

The tall guy said, "*Dê mim,*" and toothless handed the medal to his crony. The gunman kept an eye on Michael while he gently ran his thumb on the raised face. He slipped the medal into his pocket. The short dude gave Michael a grin that looked like a comedy mask.

He motioned that Michael should drop his briefs. The two men laughed at Michael's hesitation. The darkness of the evening had descended, and the air was cool. The clouds had turned blue-gray with pink underbellies. Michael trembled. He felt like the caipirinhas had swelled his bladder up to his throat. But he resolved not to give these two pricks the satisfaction of asking to pee. He tossed his underwear on the pile of clothes, and at their command, he sat his naked butt on the grass.

The short dude got into the Malibu and tried to start it. He must have seen the gas gauge because he didn't make a second attempt and said something to the gunman. The response sounded to Michael like a command. The short dude bristled and talked back. The tall guy raised his voice, and the short dude banged the steering wheel with his hand. He left the Malibu, got into the Fusca and drove away. A tingle went up Michael's neck, and his heart rate zoomed. He thought, he's going to shoot me, and he doesn't want his homie to be a witness. If I spring to my feet and run, maybe I'll surprise him and he'll miss the first shot. He looked at the sinew-lean gunman and Michael thought, I'd never outrun the bastard. Michael pressed down on his groin to keep his piss repressed, but it started, and he leapt to his feet. The urine jet sprayed like a geyser, and his captor sidestepped the stream like a juking halfback. When Michael finished, the gunman gestured he should retake his seat away from the muddy puddle. The gunman slid his butt onto the hood of the Malibu like he was tailgating at a football game. In the moonlight, his white teeth gleamed.

In a half-hour, the Volkswagen returned. The short man emerged with a red plastic gas container. His face was dark as he walked over to the Malibu, unscrewed the gas cap and dumped the gas into the tank. Michael thought, the reason he didn't kill me was because they want to steal my car and wouldn't risk the noise of a gunshot until they were ready to drive both cars away. A rush of acidic bile surged into Michael's throat. The short dude tried to start the engine without success. He popped the hood, took off the air filter and looked into the carburetor. He sniffed and touched the intake valves with his fingers. He said something to the gunman, who responded curtly. The short dude said, "*Foda*," detached the fuel line, sucked on the tube and siphoned gas into the carburetor. He spat violently, said, "*Filho da puta*," reattached the line, and went back to the driver's side. The car started.

With a nod from the gunman, the short man got out of the Malibu. He picked up Michael's clothes and threw them into the trunk, and took the driver's seat in the Volkswagen. The tall man faced Michael and aimed his pistol. Michael turned his eyes from the muzzle of the gun, and his brain whirled. This can't be happening, he thought. I ran out of gas. You don't get murdered for running out of gas. This is crazy. Michael raised his head. The open barrel was in his face. Tears squeezed from his eyes. "Mother of God, no. You don't have to kill me. I won't tell anyone. Please."

The tall man's face furrowed behind the cocked pistol. He pulled the gold medal from his pocket and looked at the Virgin Mary. His eyes rose to Michael. The gunman kissed the image and tossed the chain into Michael's lap. He uncocked the pistol and slid into the Malibu's driver seat. The Volkswagen and the Malibu's engines were gunned, and the two men sped off into the night. Michael clenched the gold chain in his fist and sobbed.

Neil Mathison

Bread and Water

The Lieutenant doesn't want to be here, not in the South China Sea, not six decks down, not outside this Navy aircraft carrier's brig, not in the Marine warder's chair behind the warder's steel desk while the warder goes to get the prisoner, one of the Lieutenant's men, a Fireman Taylor. Taylor is serving three days on bread and water. The sentence, awarded at Captain's Mast, surprised the Lieutenant. The Lieutenant didn't know bread and water was still a Navy punishment, although Taylor's crime, striking a petty officer, is severe. The Lieutenant was further surprised that he, the Lieutenant, must "counsel" the prisoner during the man's incarceration. *It's the regulation*, the XO explained. The Lieutenant has never been in the brig before and he doesn't want to be near the brig and he doesn't want to deal with Taylor or with Taylor's troubles. Lately the Lieutenant isn't his usual gung-ho self. Lately, the Lieutenant has troubles of his own.

The brig reeks: ammonia, sweat, new paint, and a smell the Lieutenant can't identify. What is it? Vomit? The temperature must be ninety degrees. A metallic light fluoresces from the overhead lamps. Swabs hang upside-down from a row of mesh-cage cells like prisoners strung up to dungeon walls. What if the ship sinks? What if there's a fire? How do prisoners get out of this place? The Lieutenant is getting a headache. For a moment he has trouble drawing his breath. Keys jangle. A hatch clangs.

Bread and water's not that bad, the XO had said. *The man gets a medical exam, a full meal, as much bread and water as he wants, and another medical exam and full meal afterwards. It's a wakeup call. A way to get the man's attention.*

Getting Taylor's attention, the Lieutenant thinks, may take more than bread and water. Taylor is stubborn as a rusted-shut dead bolt, dumber than a spanner wrench. Until now, however, Taylor hasn't been in serious trouble.

The Marine corporal who is the duty warder is crisp in his green utilities. He leads Taylor from his mesh cage. "The prisoner," the warder barks, "will stand to attention."

Taylor straightens into a semblance of military formality, gazing at the overhead through sleepy, half-lidded eyes. His head has been shaved. A pink sheen glows through the stubble on his head. Taylor's haircut exaggerates the size of Taylor's ears and makes his pale skin seem paler, his face smaller, and his thin, gawky frame gawkier. Taylor reminds the Lieutenant of the troll dolls his sister Whitney once collected, rubbery, pliable dolls with tufts of dog-gnawed hair.

"He's yours, Lieutenant," the warder says, "until his ration at 1200 hours. I'll be outside. Sing out if you need me, sir." The warder steps into the passageway. He nods apologetically. "I got to lock the hatch, sir."

The lock chinks shut.

Taylor lapses into a slouch. His eyelids droop like blinds hung in an empty window.

"Sit," the Lieutenant says.

Taylor slowly swivels his neck left, right, returning his gaze to the Lieutenant. Like a turtle, the Lieutenant thinks. "Where? Sir?"

There are no chairs except for the Lieutenant's chair.

The Lieutenant flushes. "The deck, Taylor. Sit on the deck."

Taylor swivels his gaze once more. The compartment outside the brig is no more than ten-feet square. Taylor selects a spot between two boxy transformers, under a cable run, where there's room to lean his back against the bulkhead. He lowers himself to the deck, crosses his legs Indian fashion, and slumps against the bulkhead. He rests his hands on his knees.

"Smoke?" The Lieutenant flips open a pack.

"You can't smoke in the brig – sir."

Taylor has no shoelaces in his boondocker boots, no belt in his dungarees, no ID tags hanging from his neck. A precaution. To keep the brig internees from harming themselves. The Lieutenant is surprised at Taylor's T-shirt – clean for a change. Even Taylor's shoes are shined.

The Lieutenant fiddles a cigarette between his fingers, taps it on the desk, rolls it back and forth. Does the smoking prohibition apply to officers too? "Taylor," the Lieutenant begins – he hopes his tone is appropriately somber – "have you thought about what brought you here?"

Taylor's gaze follows the cigarette rolling back and forth between the Lieutenant's hands. Taylor nods slowly.

"And what have you thought?" I sound like my father, the Lieutenant thinks, after I dented the family car or cut class or failed to make the honor role. The Lieutenant is young, only twenty-four. His father's admonitions lie close in the Lieutenant's past. Taylor's nod, the Lieutenant decides, is hopeful. "Well?"

Taylor raises his head. "I should of hit him harder."

Hopeless! What is the Lieutenant doing here? "What will your parents think?" the Lieutenant continues. What else is there to do? "About you being in the brig? About you getting bread and water?"

"Ain't got no parents."

Where's Taylor from? Was it Wisconsin? The Lieutenant tries to remember Taylor's Service Record. Was it the Dells? That's it! The Dells. The Dells, Wisonsin. The lieutenant glances at his watch. "Well, if you don't have parents, what will your girl think? You have a girl back in Wisconsin?"

"Ain't got no girl in Wisconsin."

Everybody has a girl somewhere. The Lieutenant has a girl. He hasn't received a letter from her in more than a month. His girl – her name is Angelica – his girl's last letter consisted solely of the phrase, *Take care of yourself*, a cooler message than what the Lieutenant expected, especially considering the diamond engagement ring he'd just sent her. Six carets. Purchased in the Subic Bay Navy Exchange. The ring had been returned in the envelope. Take care of yourself, she'd scrawled across the envelope face. Someone who waits for you back home, the Lieutenant believes, is an anchor, a way to hold life in place. No wonder Taylor is hopeless.

"There must be some girl somewhere," the Lieutenant says.

Taylor nods. A slow, beatific grin warms his face. "Maria."

Maria? Why is that name so familiar? Of course – the Filipino bar girl! The Lieutenant remembers her name from Taylor's Captain's Mast.

"The girl you and Petty Officer Wunderly fought over?"

Taylor's face darkens. "He called Maria a whore."

Wunderly *is* a sadistic little prick, one of the Masters-At-Arms, a ship's policeman, who revels in hassling dimwitted sailors like Taylor. But Wunderly was right about Maria. Maria is a whore.

"He said he'd screw her. He said he'd screw in front of me and the other guys."

The Lieutenant recalls that screwing Maria is *exactly* what Wunderly was doing when Taylor assaulted him with the heel of his shoe. Twelve stitches. A minor concussion. A riot followed that had to be broken up by the shore patrol. It occurs to the Lieutenant – a moment of inspiration – that the incident with Maria may offer an opportunity to put things in a context. *In context.* That's what his father used to say. If the Lieutenant proceeds cautiously.

"Taylor," the Lieutenant says, "are there bars in Wisconsin?"

Taylor's eyes blink. Open. Shut. Open. Hypnotic. The Lieutenant looks away.

"Bars where women hang out. The kind of women your mama – if you had a mama – might warn you to stay away from."

Taylor frowns. He gazes at his hands. "Murphy's Place. My aunt says we ain't to go to Murphy's Place. My aunt says they was Jezebels at Murphy's Place."

Bingo! The Lieutenant prepares to establish context.

"These women ..." the Lieutenant says, "... they ever take money? You know, to go out with a man?"

Puzzlement clouds Taylor's face. "I guess." Taylor stares at his hands.

"How about Maria? She ever take money? To go out with men?"

Taylor raises his head. "She *got* to go with guys." There's an impatient note in Taylor's voice, as if he's explaining something to a dimwitted child.

"What's the difference? What's the difference between Maria and your aunt's Jezebels?"

Taylor no longer blinks. His eyes glow with conviction. "Maria loves me."

"How do you know she loves you?"

"Maria wants to marry me."

The Lieutenant feels context slipping away. The Lieutenant remembers Angelica's visit to his parent's cottage on Cape Cod, remembers his father pulling him aside after Angelica left, remembers his father asking, *Isn't Angelica a little fast for you?* And he remembers his own unwavering faith. For a minute the Lieutenant is silent. He listens to the whine of the transformers, smells the sour odor of the brig, senses the too-close proximity of the prisoners, feels the papery cigarette in his fingers.

"Taylor," the Lieutenant says. "Is there anything you need, anything I can do for you?"

Taylor frowns. His face brightens. He reaches into his dungaree pocket and pulls out a creased envelope. "Take this to Maria, sir. When we get to Subic. Take it to Maria at the Club Flamingo."

"What do I tell her?"

"You don't tell her nothing, sir. She's waiting for it."

The warder clangs the hatch open. "1200 hours, sir."

"Okay." The Lieutenant takes the envelope. "We're done."

Later, six decks above the brig, in the privacy of his stateroom, sitting at his desk, the Lieutenant opens Taylor's envelope. A steel ring spills out. It is actually a stainless steel nut polished and smoothed and buffed until it glows like silver. The Lieutenant reaches for his lockbox. He draws Angelica's envelope from the box and empties it. Her ring – his ring – rattles across the desk. The two lie side-by-side: Taylor's soft steel, the Lieutenant's diamond, glittering, flickering, flaming with the diamond's inconstant light. It won't work – Taylor and Maria – the bar girl and the love-blind fireman. All Maria wants is a ticket to America. At least Maria *sees* what she wants: the red, white, and blue bounty of America – supermarkets and boxes of Tide detergent, Colonel Sanders and cinema multiplexes. Taylor can't see anything – except that he's finally getting laid. The Lieutenant picks up his ring. He's always surprised at how light it is. Three months pay. This is what you get. It'll never work. The lieutenant drops the diamond ring in Taylor's envelope anyway.

CARA EHLENFELDT

Portraiture

You are open, you lie on the couch, peeled
Apart like some sort of fruit or flower that
I cannot name. Your hands, darting mice,
Give life where there was stillness.
When framed properly, you are alone –
When framed perfectly, you are surrounded,
Bubbling forth everyone you know,
Resonating into the dry, empty air.
Your body is there, but your presence
Expands until emptiness is as impossible
As nothingness, and I feel you flooding
Towards me. This moment, you speak of
A thousand poems, and I listen, trying
To snatch each one from the cool night air
Before sleep dispels all feeling and thought.

NARENDRA SHARMA

Shades of Nature

KATHLEEN SPIVACK

The Story of Herself

When I die
let them say
*she knitted the story of
herself.* Let them read
what underlay the pattern,
child and stitch. A cat. And men.
How she spread her body out
to be stroked and
warm, was understood
and worn/worn out:
why not? She was a knitter/
purler; *wrote the book
you hold in your hands.*

Let them say:
*she gave all her paintings away
to friends who loved them.*
Rack upon rectangled racks,
encased squared canvases
caged on their dark shelves and
hoarded against her *who-knows-when-
some-day.* The noon-wrinkling odor
of fresh oil paint, slick under
her quick hand, her eye for
color & detail,
the squint/sketches, beaches
and travel and all those little
houses where she stayed: let them
be liberated, splendid and

squandered, the mad freedom
given away while
she still lives among them,
sun-lit, splashing the
walls of her friends. Rooms,
let them breathe:
we will remember her
by her paintings.

And as I die
let me not suffer too
much (*of a much*). Let me be
"of sound mind," approaching
the green mossy cave of goodbyes,
the fern-wind's whispered
Thank you.

KRIKOR DER HOHANNESIAN

The Horrible Band

An innocent enough beginning,
the sun a lone ornament radiant
over Ipswich Bay, pacific waters
lapping the headland with the rhythmic
slap-slap of incipient high tide. Gulls,

terns soaring in elliptical loops, nose-diving
for chum scummed in the wake of a rusty trawler
laden to the gunwales with a day's haul.
Beach roses swaying to the wisp of a breeze
off the Atlantic…a halcyon day,
this day of Independence, this day
of cannon, fireworks, of glut
in jingoistic revelry. Down the rutted path

clomps the band, *sui nomen* the Horrible Band,
warming to revelry fueled by cheap beer
and reefer. Ersatz drums—picnic coolers
and sticks of driftwood—percuss
the serenity of the afternoon, rat-a-tat
rat-a-tat,…air horns blare…desultory
explosions of pinwheels, roman candles,
screaming meemies wage war on tranquility.

A parade at dusk and a bonfire, we are told,
refuge only in the lee of the headland. Below
on the rocks spilling to the ocean a doe
lies splayed—foreleg grotesque, neck
spiraled, flies celebrating the stench of death.

I imagine her, independent, bounding with sublime
grace across the high meadow and then the moment
of instinctive horror, the fatal misstep…had she
cried out, had anyone heard? I pray for her gentle soul,
watch the sun slip into the horizon of this, her final
day. The Horrible Band heads a motley parade
of Hell's Angels rejects up the path, the music
a disjointed blather. A teenager boasts loudly
of drinking mother under the table. Dusk

collapses to darkness, a four-story funeral pyre
of kerosene-drenched palettes and old lobster crates
sets the night air ablaze in pagan bacchanal. Embers
ride the draft heading for the stars. Like Icarus

perhaps I had flown too close to the sun,
sensibilities melted in a Dantean inferno of the surreal.

Lanesville, MA
Cape Ann
July 4, 2007

Orphic Dreams

I.

You told me of your dream—
where I was to be tried, then
judged for some offense,
  no writ, no warrant, a mystery.
And when that day
of reckoning arrived I was scaling
the granite steps of a courthouse—
          it was somewhere in Armenia—
and there sat the judge,
a woman, whose eyes spoke

"you needn't fear me,
          I know why you are here…

I drop to my knees, genuflect
on stone, hands in supplication, the sum
of my life awash in a cascade
of tears cleansing the steps.

II.

And now it is afternoon, along
the New England shore, a hot summer day—
the kind that makes you want to live forever.
I am lying on grass, cool to my back,
and here is my dream. I am walking
an estuary in Carolina delta country.
Cypress and Spanish moss hang over the banks,
a cathedral enveloped by mist

rising off the water. Droplets of dew
serene, cling to my body, naked, but the air
feels eerie, haunted with tacit warning,

"if you cross the creek
there will be no going back..."

I am pulled and I dip a toe, an ankle and
now I am up to my knees, moving
toward the far bank, when I feel
a presence at my back, hackles on edge.
I sense my daughters on the bank from
whence I came. The chorus echoes:

"if you turn to look at them,
you'll never see them again..."

I am too weak, only
a silent prayer wells:

"whoever grants forgiveness,
please forgive me"

III.

They are huddled like refugees,
tiny rills of sadness on their cheeks,
their hands wave once, twice, a tentative
farewell, their eyelids droop in mourning
and now I am weeping, turning away.
An aura is suspended in the mist—though
I can't see you, I know it is you.
I feel your embrace, it holds
kindness, offers the solace I crave.
I evaporate into your arms,
we vanish in the fog, shapeless.

Waiting for the Rain

In the afflicted young
there is a phrase for it,
"failure to thrive",
a lack of interest
in their yet small worlds,
a tendency to squall more
than most – not yet have they
the words to describe.

For those of us nearing the inevitable,
the drip, drip of falling energy,
the ache in the bones, skin
cracked like a dried up arroyo
waiting for the gully-washer
that never comes. There is
a catch-all for this, too—
"ah, it's just old age."

For the aging poet it is words,
his life blood, that slowly dry up.
He searches for rock hibiscus
and pigeon-berry in his desert
of desiccated inspiration. He
hopes for the flood of afternoon rain,
the thunder-squall of words, the poem,
the arc of the rainbow at day's end.

JENNIFER JEAN

Hunger

1.

In early fall when cupboards were empty,

or when mom stuck a fridge-note on a little meal
of pork chop and potato—
again
telling me to cook it
for my older brother, Joey—

I got out
hungry.

2.

In early fall some builders tried to build
townhomes too near our concrete
welfare rentals.
Every day the structure

got knocked into place,
some of us would creep up, past curfew,
hungry to break
into that unlit skull, that lux
timber cage.

Two or three flirts
bounced around "security,"
giggled their guard down,

while kids from our building toured blind
over storied scaffolding. We'd trip
through hingeless door jams,
understanding ourselves as unseen
targets, as fun-takers

from a crew of fun-makers
chucking bricks and cement chunks,
molding and four by fours

at air. All us
flip-flop girls in tanks
huddled, shuffled, clenched
elbows, felt for hands and names
as plywood shanks
harpooned past our temples.

Pocked up Brian Etsel had a mean thrust,
and he hardly hid his jerky huffing in the absolute
dark.

3.

Then clods came at us—
one smacking my bared navel. The dirt fixing
into sunken folds,
making me itch
that old wound. We shielded
our glossed and blue-shadowed faces from the sting
of those rude strikes.

Some girls squealed and panted
as if bullets sprayed.

4.

You can't get me, Tasha bluffed.
Oh yeah? Mike grabbed at her, got flesh, got
me—swung and dipped me in a tango trance,
as if he'd plant a kiss. He

smeared a crap-clod over my mouth, said,

Another one bites
the dust.

5.

My brother Joey always cracked
jokes—his eyes fixing
on some broke line he had to walk
to live among the building's boys.

He had to be their four-eyed,
faceless croupier—earning his living

never winning. In those home-free nights,

he back-kicked propped up sheet metal—
made it wobble and twang,
made it be the thing

that bent.

6.

But why should I feed him?
I'd ask my friends.
Why should I keep that dolt from skating
unfilled pools?

7.

I never
		picked up the rebar and whacked
at stained glass, like knocked-up Erica.

I didn't
		yip yip yip like Anton the shrimp,
steel toe stomping
like a punk-monkey.

I liked that liar,
Liar Mike, the guy blocking the exit—
calling out, *Tasha!*
Dinnertime!

She'd grab my arm, say,
Sorry. Thought you were a brick.
She might have thrown me at him—
hunger made me

a spike. *Eat me, Mike!* we said, *Talk more*
crap so I can find you...

8.

I wasn't always like this.

One weekend that summer I wolfed
white mellow peaches
from the market at snow-fed Big Bear Lake
near a lent log cabin built—by the friend
of a friend of a friend
of my mom—between sugar pines.

That was flesh.
That was fluent sweet
rushing like a brook along life lines,
over pulse points...

That was luck—
to have wrapped myself around a true
rupture.

iWarriors

The image shook as Amar tried to hold his hands steady. He shifted left and then right, and finally centering in the small digital screen was the figure of a man, gravely injured or dead, lying face down in the street. From a concrete building across the way, a long piece of rebar reached out and tried to pull the wounded man to safety. The rebar came from an open doorway, from which the shadow of a man laid across the tile floor.

Amar took a deep breath and clicked *"video."*

He watched through the screen as the piece of rebar finally hooked the wounded man's upper arm and began to drag him toward the shelter of the building. But the wounded man rolled and the piece of rebar had to come back and find another place to hook. The end of the rebar was conveniently bent like a horseshoe, and reaching across the body, it found a grasp beneath the wounded man's arm, and again, the rebar began to drag the wounded man toward the shelter of the doorway on the far side of the street. All the while Amar focused on keeping the image centered in the small digital screen, and keeping his hands steady.

He stood in a building foyer, out of the sights of the sniper, with both feet planted shoulder width apart and his arms straight out before him. He could hear someone yelling down the street, but he could not make out the words. A distant gunshot caused him to flinch but he quickly re-centered the image and resumed his stance. Slowly, the rebar worked, pulling, tugging, slipping, reaching back for another grasp, and finally heaving the injured man to the safety of the building.

Amar looked at the face of his smartphone, touched the *save* option, watched for the confirmation, and then tucked the phone in his blue jeans. He disappeared into the doorway behind him, hurried through an empty corridor, and came out on the opposite street a block away. He looked in both directions, and when he saw that all was clear, he sprinted down the sidewalk in the opposite direction from which he had come.

After three blocks he slowed to a brisk walk, turned a corner, and stopped mid-block beneath an open window.

Amar made a whistling sound. A head popped out from the window, looked in both directions down the street, and then down at Amar. Amar tossed the smart phone up, and the man in the window caught it using both hands. The man disappeared into the window, the window closed, and Amar walked inconspicuously down the street toward his apartment.

Inside the building, the smartphone was hurried down a hallway to a secluded room. There, was a makeshift office designed to receive and transmit video dispatches to the media world outside. Two men sat at two tables with a laptop computer in front of each of them. The smartphone was promptly handed over to the nearest computer operator, who promptly connected it to a USB cord, and with a stroke of the keyboard, the video was uploaded onto the laptop computer. A webpage was opened, a message link was clicked, and the man began typing in English. The other two men watched over his shoulder as the message formed on the screen:

"Freedom fighters try to rescue fallen protester, shot by Assad's henchmen, in Hama, Syria. 4th August, 2011."

Using the mouse, the man attached the video to the email, clicked the send button, and the message was sent out via satellite internet. The recipient's email address - *Al Jazeera News* - flashed back on the screen, confirming the message had been successfully sent.

The three men looked at one another and exchanged congratulatory smiles.

***

Amar entered his apartment to find his room-mate, twenty-six-year old Murhaf Rahman, in the kitchen fixing lunch; a sandwich of pita bread, humus, and meat. Leaning against the counter was an AK-47, recently smuggled in across the Turkish border, compliments of Turkey's Military High Command.

"I told you I don't want guns in here," Amar said.

Murhaf took the rifle, opened the kitchen closet, and tucked the gun away inside. He then resumed fixing his sandwich.

"We having a good day, *brother?*" Murhaf asked.

"Yes, it has been a good day, *brother,*" Amar replied.

Brothers they were, but not in blood. It was the five-month-old rebellion that bonded them; though they had differing views on exactly how the rebellion should be conducted. Murhaf, a member of the *Free Syrian Army*, was committed to taking up arms while Amar, one among a self-proclaimed group of internet warriors, relied on technology and internet connectivity in their fight against Damascus. Here, in a country where foreign media was banned and local coverage was severely restricted, the only way the outside world could see what was really happening in Syria was through the efforts of Amar and his comrades. Until now, the best they could do was upload grisly homemade videos onto *YouTube*; of victims mangled by gunfire, and other unsubstantiated events, via makeshift satellite transmitters or flash cards smuggled across the border into Turkey.

Despite their different ways, Amar and Murhaf were both freedom fighters; until then, known to the World's media as the *Opposition*—Syria's anti-regime protesters.

But Amar knew it was not really an opposition, it is the whole of Syrian society.

"We will be meeting this evening," he said in English. "I would like you to come."

Murhaf was surprised at the invitation since the two had frequently exchanged their opposing views on the rebellion.

"I want you to see what we do. I want you to meet Hazem," Amar continued.

"I think it would be a waste of time," Murhaf said.

"He is a wise man. If you hear his words…"

"Why? Because he speaks English?"

"No, because he speaks words that make better sense than any man I know."

"I'm sorry. I do not understand this kind of warfare," Murhaf said.

"How do you know unless you come and listen?"

"It is time wasted."

Amar stared at Murhaf in a pleading effort. "Perhaps you will find it in yourself to join us, *brother?*"

Murhaf said nothing.

"We will be meeting at the safe house on Friday," Amar said.

And he said nothing more.

On Friday the meeting took place as scheduled. Hazem Saleh, the leader of this rogue band of cell-phone journalists, stood at the front of an improvised meeting room. He was a distinguished-looking man, middle-aged with graying hair and a graying beard, and was dressed in a business suit which had obviously not been pressed for some time. He had worked as a media supervisor for the Syrian Center for Media and Freedom of Expression before it had been completely abolished by Damascus, and had been a senior foreign correspondent for BBC World News, before foreign news had been outlawed. He had since utilized his skills to organize and orchestrate media coverage to the outside world, trying to bring some sense of professionalism to a band of gypsies.

There were several men seated in metal folding chairs, among them Amar. Near an opened widow was a portable, twenty-inch satellite dish pointed skyward. It had been skillfully mounted on a camera tripod and positioned far enough from the window so that it could not be seen from the street below. A wire ran from it to a box of wires on a nearby table.

Hazem addressed the men in Arabic.

"It is a good day, my friends, my brothers. The sun is out. We are alive. And the fate of Syria is securely in our hands. The longer the revolution lasts, the better chance we have for freedom."

A noise came from the rear of the room and all eyes turned back to see Murhaf standing in the doorway.

"Welcome, brother," Hazem said.

Amar greeted Murhaf with a smile and offered him a seat, but Murhaf found a place against the back wall where he leaned his shoulder and remained silent.

Hazem took the laptop, opened it, turned it on, and set it on the table. As the screen lit up he turned it so that all in the room could see. He then clicked on a desktop icon.

On the screen appeared *Al-Jazeera English* showing grainy images from a mobile phone of detainees being beaten by Syrian soldiers. The reception, which was poor to begin with, went hazy and then vanished. A young man sitting next to Hazem near the front of the room got up and played with the satellite dish until the feed came back and the images came in clearly.

Hazem clicked on another icon and a second video began to play. Amar quickly recognized it to be the video stream he had captured on his smartphone; that of the long piece of rebar reaching out for the wounded man. Along the bottom of the screen within a blue stripe were the words, *BBC Worldwide News.* The announcer, a very British-looking, well-dressed woman with blonde hair, spoke in King's English: "President Bashar Assad's bloody crackdown on protesters has taken an ominous turn over the weekend. In the city of Hama, an armored attack on thousands of protesters killed at least

150 civilians on Sunday. There were also reports of attacks by the army in at least four other cities with dozens more killed. The increasing violence has raised eyebrows in the West. The number of people killed in the bloody repression of an uprising against the government in Syria has now risen to at least thirty-five thousand, awakening leaders of the international community…"

"It is exactly what we need!" Hazem said. "To open the eyes of the *West*, to find support of the international community. It is our *path*, our *way* to freedom, and we are the window to the world, God's spies on earth." Hazem's eyes searched and found Amar. "And thanks be to brother Amar, whose courage and steady hand has brought us this recognition."

Hazem turned back to the computer screen and watched for a moment as the announcer continued. "Once-friendly nations have now criticized President Bashar al-Assad…" the announcer's voice spoke. "And French President Nicolas Sarkozy has demanded his Syrian counterpart Bashar al-Assad to step down for overseeing massacres of his own people."

Hazem gazed across the room, his eyes smiling. They had secured an audience in the Arabic world already with many news reels airing on *Al Arabiya*. Now, they had found an English audience as well.

Hazem turned the screen off.

"It is success, my friends," he said. "It is a new milestone. Now it's only a matter of time and Assad will fall." His eyes glanced down at the table-top. "And today, we have been afforded a new tool to advance our crusade."

On the table were two small boxes. Hazem took one of the boxes, turned it over and held it so that all could see the image on the cover. It was an iPhone 4. He turned the box to its side and showed the printed words, "*Apple - iPhone 4S*." He flipped it and began to open it, and half way through the process he tossed the second box into Amar's lap.

Amar looked up and smiled, and promptly followed suit, opening the second box as well.

"It has enhanced camera and video," Hazem spoke, now holding the iPhone in his hand. He waited for it to light-up. "Much higher resolution, thirty frames per second, longer battery life, and enhanced HD quality. With this, we can take media-quality video."

He turned the iPhone so that all could now see the lit touchscreen.

"CNN... Anderson Cooper... here we come!"

The room erupted with applause.

In the back of the room, Murhaf stood restlessly. He saw no reason to celebrate. *It was not the path,* he thought. A new phone, sure it was nice, but it was no match to the weaponry of Assad's regime.

"No rebellion was ever won without violence," he spoke loudly.

All eyes turned back at him.

"It is silliness to believe you can win a war with a phone."

The men exchanged glances and then turned their eyes up to Hazem. They all knew Murhaf and knew of his resistance to their media-focused rebellion. After all, Murhaf was a member of the emerging *Free Syrian Army*, whose doctrine was dedicated to the use of force, not to diplomatic change. It was his kind that brought great worries to men like Hazem, not that anyone questioned the FSA's dedication to the revolution. It was sectarian war that troubled him; the fear that Murhaf and his comrades, in their quest for liberty, would push the country into a civil war; a war that, once started, could not be stopped and would result in the destruction of Syria.

"Then our rebellion will be the first," Hazem said boldly, finally breaking the silence.

"Assad will not fall to an image on a smartphone," Murhaf replied fearlessly. "Ask the people of Libya."

"Maybe it was true in Libya. But this is Syria. And we are Syrian people, and if we can find justice through diplomatic means… through peaceful means, without Syrians spilling the blood of Syrians, shouldn't we choose peace?"

Murhaf looked cold suspicion at all of them. He was a believer in self-reliance; in the one truth that all things that must be changed, must be changed by one's will to resist. Defiance was the *path*, he thought. Waiting for a diplomatic resolution, requesting help, especially from the Western World, was not only hypocritical but just short of cowardice.

"A brother falls and you photograph it?" Murhaf asked. He paused, glanced over all of them, and then repeated his words, "A brother falls and you photograph it? You photograph the blood of your mothers and fathers, the blood of your brothers and sisters, and your children?" Again pausing, looking over the silent group. "When will you fight back? If not today, if not tomorrow, then when?"

"We fight back, everyday," Hazem refuted calmly. "With a picture that paints a thousand words and a pen that is mightier than the sword. And with the will of the people, and the will of the *Creator*, we will succeed."

They were elegant words, Murhaf thought, but overused in the course of human history and not worthy of a response. He remained silent.

"It is through international pressure and intervention," Hazem continued. "With the might of the West and the support of the Arabic states, Assad will crumble." He looked at Murhaf. "Are you for the revolution?"

"Of course."
"Then take this weapon," Hazem said.

To the surprise of the other men in the room, Hazem held out the second iPhone, offering it to Murhaf.

Murhaf stared at it.

Hazem's arm extended. "Here. Take it. This is our implement of war."

For a moment Murhaf's eyes remained locked on the iPhone. The other men watched, waiting to see what he would do. *It is such a small and simple device,* Murhaf thought. *Not a device for overcoming oppression or stopping tanks from rolling over defenseless protestors.*

He shook his head. "I don't believe in the power of the pen," he said. "I believe in the power of the sword. Give the phone to someone who believes in it."

Hazem slowly withdrew his arm.

The meeting ended, uneventful and Hazem took Murhaf's advice, later presenting the second iPhone to young Rami Ibrahim who had demonstrated bravery and cleverness in capturing aerial-like shots of protest-busting soldiers from rooftops. There was the normal handing out of assignments, and because there was to be a great demonstration in Assi Square in three days, Hazem took special care to coordinate full coverage of the event. He had a large map of the square, had sectioned it off into quadrants, and assigned the men to strategic spots within the plaza.

After everyone had left, Amar and Murhaf walked back to their apartment silently.

"Why come to the meeting at all if you are going to cause problems?" Amar finally spoke.

"A man educated in the West?" Murhaf mumbled to himself. He had a little half-smile he used to show disdain, and he wore it now. "It is only because he was educated in the West that you trust him."

"Why do you say that?"

"Since when do Syrians follow *Western* ways and *Western* words?" Murhaf said and then stopped. "*Crusade?* Whose crusade?"

"It is because his *way* is the just way, under the eyes of God," said Amar. "Some Syrians resist violence. Why have a problem with that?"

"You have forgotten your American history," Murhaf huffed. "Democracy never came from peace. It comes from war. It is a fact of history. All great Nations have risen from blood. If Lenin waited for a peaceful demonstration, Russia would still be ruled by Czars. If Libyans relied on iPhone images, Gaddafi would still be laughing. And if you turn the other cheek now, Assad will roll over you with his tanks."

"Murhaf, I pray that you do not destroy us."

"No war was ever won by peaceful protest. The free people of Syria and its mujahideen will overthrow Assad, but we will not do so with an iPhone."

***

Three days had passed and Murhaf's prophetic words had rung true. The safe house had been raided by government soldiers and their esteemed leader, Hazem Saleh, had been dragged off and killed. Much of their equipment had been seized or destroyed. The laptops, which contained email lists of outside contacts on their hard-drives, were taken away by the regime's intelligence service for deciphering. Any man who had used his name in any email, in anyway, was now a hunted fugitive.

Hazem could not be replaced, but as they had done in the past, the rebel effort regrouped and refortified. As safe houses were raided and destroyed, new ones popped up. As equipment was seized or destroyed, new equipment was donated or smuggled in from Lebanon or Turkey along the many smuggling paths which linked one safe house to another. And as leadership was lost, new leadership was found.

The massive demonstration in Assi Square had begun in the morning hours as scheduled, but had turned deadly by early afternoon. The number of demonstrators had swelled into the thousands, too many for the government to stand by and tolerate, so tanks and armored vehicles rolled in and seized the square. Some of the activists tried to stop the advancing armored columns with makeshift barricades, but they were no match to the military might. Amar had watched, and had filmed as the demonstrators scattered and fell back. Some of them, the fighters like Murhaf, had stayed in the square, throwing stones at armor. But the regime released their snipers, and their mafia-like gunmen known as *"shabiha"* who operated as hired guns for the regime, and they began to systematically cut down any pocket of resistance.

Amar stood back from it all in a small building alcove. He held his iPhone out steady before him and filmed what unfolded before him.

From behind the barricade, he saw a man stand up and raise his fist at the armored vehicles.

"Freedom forever, despite you Assad!" yelled the man.

The man was promptly shot in the head, fell to the ground, and his blood ran in the street and glistened in the sunlight.

Another man who sprang to his aid was also shot, and he fell diagonally, cross-bodied over the first.

"Now Assad," Amar said to himself disdainfully. "How will you explain this?"

Another demonstrator threw a rock which bounced off the windshield of one of the armored vehicles. The rock was answered by a volley of machinegun fire, but the man had wisely ducked down quickly and escaped injury, for the moment.

Then the barricade was overrun by the *shabiha*, who came from all directions with clubs and guns and riot gear, and began beating, indiscriminately, any activist who failed to flee. Those who had fallen to the ground were kicked and dragged back to the armored vehicles.

Amar watched and filmed as another demonstrator fell to his knees with men over him flailing with their clubs, striking him against his arms which he held up to protect himself until his arms could no longer take the beating and fell to his side, and then his head was bare and unprotected and the clubs came against his head until finally he dropped, lifeless, and was dragged off with the others.

"And this? It is Islamic extremists? The world will now see Assad! The world will now see how you really are… and all your lies!"

It is brutality, Amar thought, and in that moment he reflected back on Murhaf's words. *It is true… It is I standing by as my brother falls. It is I watching the spilling of Syrian blood and doing nothing about it. Is it reprehensible? No! It is necessity. We film, not because we like it, but because it is the path to freedom. It is the only way to defeat this monster.*

Then, through the small digital screen, Amar saw one of the government thugs turn and look his way. Some of the other militia turned as well, and before Amar knew it, one of them had his rifle raised and pointed at him. Amar quickly ducked back into the alcove, breathing heavily. When he poked his head back around the corner, he saw the remaining demonstrators fleeing in all directions, and the *shabiha* coming his way. Amar turned and ran, as hard and fast as he could.

In the minutes that followed, Amar could not remember much, only running fast and breathing hard, until he was beyond the earshot of the carnage. He found himself in a protective alcove trying to catch his breath. He was sweating heavily. His mouth was stiff and dry from fear and from all the running. He looked down and realized his leg was shaking and he held his hand against it until it stopped.

He stood there and watched as the people ran past until there were no more. He snuck a glance around the corner and down the street. The street was deserted. He knew he needed to build his courage to return to the square. It was there that were the journalistic gems that would turn the tide of this rebellion.

"You must be brave," he said to himself.

He looked again and saw no one. Then he stepped out into the street and began walking forward, filming images of burned buildings and rubble-strewn streets empty of people, yet four blocks away from the square.

A man emerged from behind a building and yelled as he ran past. "It is not safe, brother! Save yourself for another day."

Amar continued, and another man came running past.

"Turn back," the man yelled. "The entire Syrian Army is coming."

Ahead Amar heard distant screams and gunfire, but could see nothing. He ducked into another building alcove, debating whether to continue or not.

"It is time for war, brother," a voice said behind him.

Amar turned and saw Murhaf standing there, leaning against the wall. His AK-47 was in one hand and a can of Red Bull in the other. Murhaf smiled, brought the can of the Red Bull to his lips, and tilted his head back to get the last drop. He then tossed the skinny can to the ground.

"Come brother," he said. "I will help you get your pictures."

Amar was surprised to see his friend, but relieved nonetheless. In the midst of all this chaos, he was not alone.

He nodded his head.

Murhaf peeked around the wall of the building, down the street. Then he led Amar across to the other side, keeping tight to the walls of the buildings as they proceeded north toward the square.

They zigzagged from one side of the street to the other, keeping clear of the sniper fire that rotated from alternating rooftops.

Ahead, the street broadened into a boulevard.

Murhaf ducked into a building foyer, the architectural design of which offered a protective alcove.

"It will be more dangerous to cross further down," Murhaf said.

Amar nodded.

Murhaf held his rifle in a defensive position and peered around the corner. The protruding façade of the building allowed for a commanding view in both directions. Now he could see the last barricade, a half-kilometer ahead, and he could see movement behind it. The last of the demonstrators, those who had pulled back from the square, had assembled yet another wall of toppled carts and lobby furniture, beyond which it was difficult to see because the air was filled with teargas and smoke.

Murhaf never liked this street. It was too big, and too wide, he thought. It was the financial district, built to show political might. It reminded him of all those who were in power. It was a street for the government elite, he thought, not for the common person. But he knew they needed to cross this street in order to be on the south side of the square, and this was as good a place as any.

Ahead they heard gunfire, and they saw a demonstrator running to the opposite side of the street. Another gunshot sounded and a bullet ricocheted off the pavement near the man as he made a last leap onto the sidewalk and into a building. Murhaf looked up and saw the dark outline of a head just above the roofline on the opposite side of the street. As soon as he saw it, the head went down.

The demonstrator, safely in the building, peeked out a broken window and then disappeared.

Murhaf looked at Amar. "It's our turn," he said.

Amar nodded.

Murhaf looked up at the roofline and saw nothing. "Let's go."

"Okay."

And without further delay, they bolted across the street, and as they did, midway through, something fell to the ground. It clanged to the pavement, and when they looked back, they saw the iPhone there in the middle of the street, lying there exposed like a flayed rabbit.

Amar reached into his pocket, disbelieving it had fallen out. His pocket was empty. In his mind, he was thinking of all the images it contained; among them the most striking video recordings of Assad's brutal tactics taken to date.

"I must get it," he said quickly.

"Wait."

"I must get it," Amar said again, and without hesitation, he began to move forward.

"Wait!" Murhaf said, holding his hand out against Amar's chest.

Murhaf already knew of the sniper above them. He checked the buildings down the street. Along the roofline of a tall building on the left, another head showed itself. The head stayed up for a second and then went back down. *That makes two,* he thought.

He huddled there for a moment, thinking.

"There's another one up there," he said, motioning with his head.

Amar looked up but saw nothing.

They looked at one another speculatively. For the moment, they were safely out of the sights of the snipers; their heads and bodies were behind the wall of the building. Murhaf looked back at the cell phone shinning in the sun. There within, he thought, were the pictures to paint a thousand words. Amar looked nervous and was sweating profusely. Further down the street, Murhaf could see the last barricade with only a few remaining demonstrators behind it. There were distant sounds from the square beyond, rattling machinegun fire and distant shouting, and he could tell by the way the demonstrators were crouched down and taking cover, something was coming, something big. In his mind he made the decision to retrieve the phone, not because he preferred it over charging ahead and spilling the blood of the *Alawite* thugs, but because he knew Amar was determined to get it at any cost, and that he, Murhaf, was better equipped of the two to engage such risk.

"Stay here," Murhaf said.

Amar did not challenge.

Murhaf took one last glance at the rooftop. He saw nothing. Then he took a deep breath, gripped the AK-47 tightly in his hand, and bolted into the street.

A single shot of a sniper's rifle stopped Murhaf, mid-stride, like he'd been hit by a ghost or something. He staggered two more steps and dropped to the pavement.

"Murhaf!" Amar cried.

For a second, Murhaf tried to pull himself up. But he fell back down and he laid there flat on his back, facing up, his rifle an arm's length away from his extended hand. And now, Amar could see blood coming from beneath him and pooling in the street.

"Murhaf!"

Amar impulsively leaped into the street. He fell to one knee beside his fallen friend and looked down at Murhaf's lifeless face.

"Murhaf," he cried.

My good friend, lost now too to this uprising? The pointlessness of it struck him suddenly.

The fatigue of hopelessness showed on Amar's face. He felt himself shaking; he felt the emptiness that came from it all. *The rebellion is crumbling,* he thought.

The rattling of gunfire caused Amar's hands to impulsively grab at Murhaf's rifle. In an instant, he found himself standing alone in the street clenching an AK-47 in his hands.

A shot rang out and a bullet ricocheted off the pavement near him and when Amar looked up he saw the head again above the rooftop. Amar pulled the rifle up to his shoulder, leveled it and fired. The rifle recoiled violently, spattered out several rounds, and the head quickly dropped back down below the roofline.

The droning sound of oncoming tanks, once heard, is not soon forgotten, and now Amar heard this sound, in columns, ten-fold. *It is the sound of doom,* Amar thought. *It is the sound of military might.* He felt the vibration of the earth; he could hear the slow, steady, creaking noise, the mechanized hum of powerful engines, the clacking of tracks against pavement.

Through the smoke and haze of gunfire and teargas, he saw the tanks emerging, rumbling down the street directly toward him. The last of the brave demonstrators were now scattering from the barricade in all directions.

He looked down at Murhaf, his beloved friend, brother in the rebellion no more, the blood still fresh on his lips. Beside him lay the iPhone 4; there within, images that could change the course of the rebellion.

He felt his hands tighten on the wooden stock of the AK-47. He felt the blood welling-up in his head and the adrenaline pushing through his veins, he heard the sounds of rattling gunfire, and then he charged, into the haze, toward the advancing tanks.

Svetlana Kortchik

A Dog's Life

I retreated behind the couch and watched as she took a step forward and slapped him hard across the face. She slapped him once and then again, even harder. Her palm left two angry, red imprints on the white skin of his cheeks. He moved back and she followed him, shouting all the while. I was all too familiar with the bizarre, frightening dance that they performed every week. She would shout and he would take it. She would hit him and he would take it. She would step forward and he would step back. I trembled, trying not to look at them, focussing on her favourite painting instead, where cheerful, carefree kittens were playing happily in the garden.

Yes, she was a cat person and she made it clear every time she saw me.

She threw a glass of water in his direction and it flew past me, hitting the wall and shattering into a hundred tiny pieces. I felt some of those pieces in my fur and shook cautiously. I couldn't help myself; I whimpered, shutting my eyes in trepidation.

'You stupid dog!' she screamed, reaching behind the couch, grabbing me by the neck and yanking me out. 'Get out, both of you!' Just like she did with the glass moments before, she threw me at him, saying, 'I want you out of here by tomorrow!'

He managed to catch me, holding me carefully and stroking my shivering body. His hands were trembling.

'I didn't marry you so I would clear up after you and your mutt,' she added, walking out and slamming the door behind her.

He put me down gently and sat on the floor next to me, holding me close. Every once in a while I whined quietly as if in shock but I was glad it was over. I knew what would happen next. At first they wouldn't talk to each other and then she would cry, apologise, and swear that she loved him and that it would never ever happen again.

But it would. It always did.

He got up tentatively as if in shock himself. Picking up his keys and his phone and throwing them in his pocket, he called my name and silently we left. It was late, after midnight. We walked to the park through the softly lit streets and sat pensively on the bench, watching the lake that dimly reflected the flickering street lamps all around it. He scratched my ear and every now and then bent his head, kissing the top of my head. His face was wet, his eyes red. An hour passed, then another. His phone rang every ten minutes but he ignored it.

When the phone finally stopped ringing, we made our slow way back home, taking the longest route. All the lights were out and it was quiet. He didn't go into the bedroom, didn't check to see if she was there. Instead, he lay down on the couch, his clothes still on, his boots still on, and closed his eyes. I could sense that he was awake. He couldn't sleep and neither could I.

I wondered why, despite everything she did, despite her anger and her raised voice, through abuse and pain and heartache, he stayed with her. I watched his face as he struggled against his thoughts that were stopping him from getting much needed sleep, and suddenly knew the answer. It was love. He loved her and he would never ever leave, no matter what.

***

Just like so many times before, the fight was soon forgotten.

He brought her flowers, dozens of long stemmed red roses that she loved, and occasionally white carnations, which she said looked cute. Twice I knocked the vase over, the roses and the carnations flying in all directions, and I paused fearfully and looked at her but she only smiled. She cooked him dinner, watching him eat, her head resting on her arm contentedly, pretending not to notice when he snuck pieces of meat and cheese under the table for me. They cuddled in front of the TV for hours, and *The Office* turned into *Ugly Betty*, and *Ugly Betty* turned into *Lost*. His arms were around her and her face was buried in his shoulder. They took me for long walks in the park where they held hands and laughed happily, watching me chase ducks, geese, squirrels and run away at the first sight of a cat because cats terrified me. He chased her and they played in snow like children, giggling and excited. Then they sipped their hot chocolates by the fireplace, her curled up on his lap and me asleep by his feet.

'What would I do without you? I love you so much. I don't want to lose you,' she whispered in his ear.

And occasionally, he would beg, 'Please, let's go see someone. A couple's counsellor. Someone who can help us.' But he would say it quietly, as an afterthought. After all, everything was great.

'But everything is great,' she would say. 'We don't need help. We are happy.'

We were happy and we knew that this time everything would be different. Unlike all the other times before it, this time would last. And it did.

Until he forgot to buy the toilet paper.

Her shrill voice could be heard all over the building. I knew this because a neighbour knocked on the door, asking if everything was ok. 'Everything is great,' she shouted, slamming the door in his face. For a minute I was hoping that her voice would carry all the way to the police station around the corner. No such luck.

Unlike her, he spoke in low, defensive tones. 'What is wrong with you?' he said quietly. 'Why do you always ruin everything?'

She called him names. He was useless, hopeless, nothing but a joke.

'I'm not happy,' he said. 'All I remember when I think back on our relationship is abuse. All I see when I look at you is violence.'

I knew straightaway that he shouldn't have said that. Not now, when she was already shaking in rage, not ever. It was better not to provoke her. It was better to walk on eggshells, treading carefully and gingerly around the fragile, flimsy peace in our house. 'How dare you say that to me? I am your wife.' She bellowed in anger and punched the wall. Her favourite painting fell on the floor with a loud bang, the kittens' frozen faces staring happily at the ceiling. It startled me and suddenly I had to get away, had to find a better hiding place than the tiny space behind the couch that was always the first place where she looked for me. I dashed past them, desperately trying to get upstairs where I knew I would be safe.

Big mistake.

'You filthy mutt,' she wailed, and as if in slow motion I saw her leg move. 'I wish we got rid of you years ago.' I felt the sharp pain in my ribs before I even realised what was happening. Emitting a low whimper, I shot up the stairs and hid under the bed, shaking, praying that it was nothing but a bad dream. But the needles in my side were a dull reminder that it wasn't a dream. That it was our weekly reality.

For the first time in my life, I heard him raise his voice to her. I heard him all the way from the bedroom. 'I'm no longer in love with you,' he said and there was heartbreak in his voice. It was dull and empty. 'I am done with you. I can't do this anymore.'

He came into the bedroom and slammed the door, locking it behind him. He called my name, once, then again, and slowly, cautiously I crawled from under the bed and looked around. It was dark in the room and I could hardly see him but even in the dim light from the street lamp outside I could see tears in his eyes. My body quivering, his hands shaking, just like before, we clung to each other, frantically seeking comfort. Once in a while he would stroke me and whisper, 'It's ok. It's going to be ok.' And once in a while I would whine softly and nudge him with my nose.

Finally, he got up with a sigh and opened the window. He sat on the window sill, his body balanced precariously on the narrow strip of wood, and smoked one cigarette after another. As if in a trance, he stared at people and cars passing us by eight floors of cold concrete away. He coughed. I sat on the bed and watched him.

Half an hour passed, then an hour. He smoked and looked down. There was a timid knock, and her voice, sounding unusually remorseful and apologetic, begging him to come out, to talk to her, to forgive her one more time because she knew for sure that it would be the last time, that it would never happen again if only he gave her another chance. 'I love you,' she said. 'I love you, I'm sorry. I love you!'

Not even turning his head away from the abyss outside, he continued to smoke.

He rocked back and forth, his gaze fixated on a faraway point in the distance that I couldn't see. Misery and desperation were in his eyes. 'Don't do it, don't jump' was in mine. Finally he shook his head, chasing his thoughts away, looked at me and said, 'What would I do without you? You are the only one who knows.'

He closed the window, locking it with a key, and I breathed out in relief. He got a large bag from under the bed, placing it on the floor in front of him and pacing up and down the room as if lost in thought. He threw his things haphazardly into the bag until his side of the wardrobe was empty, until there was nothing left. Then he turned to me, his eyes broken and afraid. 'Let's go,' he said. 'You and I can no longer stay here.'

TED JEAN

Hellebore

MICHAEL COLLINS

Confession

A minister once told me   that his relationship with
    God   was like one with a person: If he was angry
    with them, he'd be angry,   but he wouldn't say that they
    didn't exist.

He obviously didn't know   he was talking to someone who tends
    to get texts   like this one with a picture of a few
    Uzis   and liquor bottles spread out on a table

with a caption that reads   *New Year's in Flint,*

never mind the one of the sign   on the highway that read
    Welcome to Flint,   to the end of which someone had
    thoughtfully added   *bitches.*

No one taught me to pray, so I learned how to laugh,

rehearsing epics like that of the basehead   so out-of-his-mind high
    he robbed a bank – then went shopping with the
    money   at the grocery store next door.

Apparently shoplifting was too obvious.

I laugh because the town I'm from   has so
    incomprehensibly   lost its entire mind   that I now
    somehow have no choice   but to be proud of it.

I laugh because Flint is a great place to be *from,*   that equips its
     children with skills   like how to use *fuck* as every part of
     speech,

throw gang signs   while hiding in your friends' basements,
     blast   rap with the doors locked, *run –* leave
     parties   just before the guns show up.

Quietly while I was growing up,   without my knowing,
     Death   became my name for God,

not the God of Love   who made no damn sense,   the wild,
     unconscious god   who lets someone pull a gun on
     you   at a stop sign for no fucking reason,   then
     drive away   laughing their fool ass off into the night –

Dear Wisdom,   around and within and between us, I'll
     suffer   no pretense of Providence   which let me leave
     where others died.

The only finality is that we each speak   within the other's
     stillness, deathsight   rendering memory to confession.

I know you're as real   as the *friend* who just split   the day
     we got jumped, then came back later   with a straight face and
     the nerve to ask,   *Are you ok?*

I yelled,   *Where the hell were you? What   could you
     possibly   have been thinking?*

When I contemplate our world   *today*, I still want to
     ask   the same thing of its Creator.

SYLVIA ASHBY

Ecdysis: Strip Tease

Is the snake surprised
when she looks in the mirror?
Does she glance back
to the discarded clothes,
the self abandoned to Goodwill?
So efficient, this ritual
of outgrowing herself:
she inches out of the pale grape,
unzips the browned banana peel.
A painless transmutation
this sloughing off—
she merely strips
into something more comfortable.
Then slithers away
moist and flamboyant
snug in her ready-to-wear:
the drab cast-offs, that dreary record
of old wounds, forgotten.
Slithers away
smug, born-again,
a sequined burlesque queen.
Simple reptile magic.

Options

Why should I let some smartass
sixteen-year old daughter
tell me how to organize my life?
When I can always ask Abby—
(Dear Abby, I've read your column for many years....)
Or consult my horoscope in the daily papers:
"Study your wardrobe. Make sure it's right."
Maybe dig up Grandma's old Ouija board
or try to decipher I Ching.
Why not visit Sister Sophia, Espiritualista;
perhaps confer with Delta Foxe, Reader & Guide;
extract a sliver of future from a fortune cookie?

Or write poems.

Richard King Perkins II

Reflections on Poetry Daily

(I'm reading "Poetry Daily— 366 Poems from
the World's Most Popular Poetry Website" which is
sort of like bragging that you've been less unemployed
than anyone else on your block.

Upon opening, I see the book is meant to be read like
a journal of daily reflections, one poem for each day
of the year. But instead of starting out at January 1st,
I page forward to my daughter's birthday for fun.

I'm disappointed with the poem. That momentous day
in April should be filled with all things wondrous and grand,
not memorialized with strange neck moles and teeth
falling out of faces.

Next, I turn back a couple of weeks to my wife's
birthday, and I think she would be pleased. A Mars/Venus
poem deftly pointing out the superiority of the female mind.
My wife does not need a poem to confirm this, however.

Finally, I turn back a few more weeks to my birthday and
it's a fine little piece working its poetry magic so that I must
reread to see how it was accomplished but now I'm
distracted by the half-dozen parenthetical asides
gremlinizing the workings of this verse.

I don't think parentheses belong in poetry at all— I mean,
if it doesn't work as an inclusive piece of the writing's flow
then it probably should have been edited out of the poem
altogether. Don't you agree?)

MICHELLE HARTMAN

Let Things Happen to Me

> desperate prayer
as chapped hands lift another
cheap plate from billowing suds
every car horn outside kitchen window
a luxury liner whisking her to Morocco
every siren announces a squad car
rock hard young men intent to rescue
her from deliciously shuddery doom

glass bottles rattle at grocery store
cast imaginative image in freezer door,
Irish swain —white tie and tails—
and herself, sitting on milk cart's rear step
singing, *Raggle Taggle Gypsy*
and *Steal Away*
sharing a quart of homogenized
as antidote against hangovers

anything at all as long as it's different
exciting and soon
as long as there are lingering looks,
audacious assignations
oh, to be a long legged
Toulouse Lautrec woman
dreamy minx, vaguely drawn
but definitely dissolute
able to swoon gracefully
a delicate Camille, in these
days of Valkyries

faster, more ardent the prayers
fly into empty skies
more days marching
on drudgery powered treadmill
until last warm evening bath
red chiffon swirls around her
wrapping her curves
split up the arms—
leg bent—thigh exposed
alabaster white as the tub
as the steps he tap dances
down to kiss her hand
and waltz her into oblivion

in progress

at first I thought he didn't
want to know me

after years in the talons
of his harpy wife

I realized, no, I didn't
want to know him

a father who could leave
one breath to the next

committed suicide
when I was thirteen

life tore down every wall
I constructed

until I understood it was me
I didn't want to know

so word by word
sentence by sentence

I compose myself

ANN HOWELLS

Piney Point Marina

An osprey floats above,
perusing riffled water.

Summerfolk are gone:
sleek polished boats,
sleek polished faces.

Pop music no longer
flutters crisp, white curtains.

The river, flat and somber,
closed for the season.

At Evan's Seafood,
two old watermen eat—
oyster stew and saltines.
They do not speak,
allow even this rustic décor
to fade into battered table,
scuffed linoleum, bent-backed wife—
three years gone—filling bowls
from a simmering kettle.

Eyes look beyond
a quiet Patuxent ebbing
to Chesapeake, to Atlantic;
they skim on skipjack-sails
toward a sun that bleeds
into the sea.

Fig Trees

Reading Naomi Nye's "My Father and the Fig Tree"
I find her father much like my grandfather
who planted fig trees behind his home on Chesapeake Bay.
Their leaves are large, rough and thick-fingered
like his calloused hands. The trees small
and gnarled as himself. Showy roses, peonies and sweet pea
that scramble exuberantly over fence and gatepost
belong to my grandmother—the fig trees, to him,
bearing plump green teardrops he gently twists free, in season,
each bleeding a single milky droplet,
until one, two, three peck baskets overflow. Unlike Naomi's father,
he is not a voluble man, but his dim blue eyes
brighten in anticipation. He eats a few,
teeth scraping the soft seedy flesh from the skin.
They are sweet but less satisfying than bonbons.
His joy is not in the fig but in preserves his wife prepares;
jars of seed-flecked sienna carefully sealed with paraffin
line her larder. He consumes half a jar
each day—a man with a sweet tooth and
overwhelming need for routine. When shelves sag,
well-weighted with fig preserves,
when he has work to occupy his hands,
all is right with the world.

ZVI A. SESLING

Where the Red Hair Came From

for BG

Where did the red
hair come from

Certainly not from the Irish
where the past never was

A Cossack you say, a woman
who was forced upon

Her child with new genes
and chromosomes to pass on

And pass on three generations
or more until you stand naked

In front of yourself to see the
past that made you, the future yours to choose

Buried in Ohio

Not dead, just living hell
Youngstown is a burnt out
shell, Cleveland the brunt
of jokes, Cincinnati is too
close to Kentucky and
Columbus is where leftovers live
We escape our past, but it
does not escape us
we still think Ohio – it was
pleasant once when cities
were alive, belched smoke
and flame, opened their
hearts and minds to the ships,
made love to the sky and open
space
Now it is buried in lost dreams,
forgotten heroes, a certain
rigor mortis of ideas and morals
loss of direction, a corrupt
stream of consciousness
a driverless bus hurtling toward
the river or the tunnel of emptiness

Teach Me to Hear Mermaids Dance

Title and first line from *Song* by John Donne

Teach me to hear mermaids dance
To hear the moon laugh
Teach me to see stars juggle
To hear mountains whisper
Teach me the snake's soprano song
And to hear sparrows cough
Teach me all of this
Then teach me more

VIRGINIA BACH FOLGER

The Queen of England

It's 1953, and I'm filling in
the deep blue sash on her dress in my
coronation coloring book,
my secret is that I want to be
the Queen of England.

It seems as easy as breathing—after all,
you're born to it. I don't know about the hours
she practiced wearing the heavy jeweled crown
while sitting at her desk or reading
the daily newspaper.

I don't know about the four leaf clover
her dressmaker secretly embroidered
among the flowers stitched on her gown, each one
representing a nation over which
she would thenceforth reign,

sewing that lucky talisman precisely
where her left hand would naturally fall
throughout that day, unknowingly brushing
against it to assure and reinforce,
to protect and save the Queen.

I only know how the jewels sparkle,
how her dress billows as the liquid silk
of its train marks her path. My small hand
finds the crayon marked gold and finishes
coloring in the crown, still wishing
that I was the Queen of England.

Spirals

She asks a question, again,
minutes after I've already answered it twice.
I shout my reply. She's nearly deaf.
Long pauses searching for a name or a word
she calls the phone the camera or the radio.

I slow to match my mother's shuffling feet;
my hips ache with the effort of snail-like steps,
my throat cracks with shouting, my patience flags.
I'm with you, she says. *I'm here*, I shout back.

I mourn our losses:
her halting steps
my slowing pace
repeated questions
unheard answers
erased memories

We spend time and health
stumbling toward the end
that comes both too late
and too soon.

Robert

He's Robert, the blind brother
the one who chooses not to see
not to see the orange burst of autumn leaves
against October's brilliant sky
not to see softness of the toddler's hand
as it reaches against the piano keys
not to see disappointment in an elderly
mother's eyes as he turns away.

He's Robert, the deaf brother
the one who chooses not to hear
not to hear the chickadee
chirping in the winter pines
not to hear the giggling
of three small grandchildren
not to hear the mumblings of an aged parent
talking to herself when he is gone.

He's Robert, the mute brother
the one who chooses not to speak
not to praise the rising of the morning sun
as it breaks horizon line
not to welcome the tumbling children
scrambling off the bus
not to ask the frail old woman
Mom, is there anything you need?

He's Robert, the crippled brother
the one who chooses not to move
the one who sits bound by his own chains
He's Robert, the brother who chooses
not to see, not to hear, not to speak
He's Robert, first always Robert
He's Robert, just Robert, only Robert
He's Robert, the blind brother.

LAWRENCE KESSENICH

Meditation

Cupped hands blooming on my lap
I re-integrate my island self with the
coastline from which I'm prone to
detach, like a man floating on a raft.
We once belonged to the sea, but now
we draw the wind that sweeps across
the land into our lungs. If we choose
to estrange ourselves from the billions
who breathe with us, we float further
and further away from who we are.
So, I sit, seemingly alone, but in fact
finding my way back across an ocean
to the dry land where my tribe abides.

A Small Celebration

Six hours before, I'd found myself
perched on a sheer rock face, staring down
a forty-five degree angle at an indifferent valley,
terrified of going higher, knowing I could not

go back. Suspended there, in hiking boots
fresh from the box and sweat-soaked t-shirt,
I'd faced the little coward inside myself and,
murmuring a prayer, started back up.

Now, in Al's back yard, tiny white lights
hover among the grape leaves on the arbor
like fireflies. The table is strewn with red
limbs and bodies of lobsters, with fat green
champagne bottles sleeping on their sides.

In my satiated haze, blistered feet cooling
in soft grass, I'm mildly proud, a greenhorn
who at least did not embarrass himself, who
comes by his champagne and lobster honestly.

Explorer

Department store bra ads were my only way in
to the *verboten* landscape of the female form.
No graphic sex education books, no casual
nudity on cable TV, no Internet porn,
not even *Playboy* at the barber shop—my mother

cut my hair. Up alone at dawn, I'd clip the wire
that bound the papers, spread out a copy on the floor
and turn its folio pages like an explorer
examining a book of maps. And there it would be,
a half-page of half-naked women, the round tops

of their hillock breasts rising above their bras, which
concealed topographical features I couldn't
begin to imagine. I was Cortez on his peak in Darien,
DeSoto reaching the Atlantic, Brûlé coming upon
Niagara Falls. But this was the landscape of

eternal damnation. Each moment of carnal knowledge
gained from exploring those half-revealed breasts was
a hot stamp of sin on the passport of my soul, which
only confession could remove. And yet, the heat
was irresistible, my body spoke with more

conviction than my Catholic soul, demanded
I discover what lay on the other side of
the hills that rose above those newsprint bras—
even if turned out to be the road to hell.

Grace

Over a glass of red wine, Marcus listened
to my story of abandonment by
traveling companions, empathetically
nodding in the right places, reflecting
my outrage. Mildly drunk, I ended up

on the back of his moped, which struggled
to carry both of us out into the chilly
French countryside. He took the brunt
of the cold, as I clung to his warm
back. We went to a roadhouse

miles from town, crammed with tiny tables
and jazz lovers, a Django Reinhardt-like
trio swinging in the corner. A cheap
bottle of local wine later, we were back
on the moped heading for Marcus's place.

We had to share his double bed, but I
thought nothing of it, having shared a bed
with my brother all my childhood.
I fell asleep, woke to Marcus at my
back, hand snaking over my thigh.

I've never been with a man, never
felt the desire, and though I needed love
desperately that night, I let fear get in
the way. Some would say I avoided
sin, but I know his love was a gift

I refused, like the man on a rooftop
in the joke about the flood, who refuses
a skiff, a speedboat and a helicopter,
waiting for God to save him.

A Brief Biography of Bill
In loving memory of William How

He held a beach stone gently
as he held a child's hand, listened

to a conch shell with the same
alert interest he showed friends.

For him, it was all a gift—
mineral, vegetable or

animal, the cry of a gull
eloquent as a mourning

prayer, soaring tree trunk
a direct line to God.

He understood the terror of
storms, endured them as a child,

led others through them as a man,
heart growing with each heart he touched.

It is as difficult to comprehend
a world without him as to

imagine a world without sun
highlighting wave tops, without breezes

ruffling pine boughs, without
a blue sky wide enough

to absorb our sorrows
and smile back at us every day.

LOGAN SEIDL

What America Is Doing to Baseball, Kids, and Other Stuff

Yesterday I won the World Series, and then bowled a 278.
The day before I was in a rock band that toured the world,
and sold out stadiums all while playing cover songs. And today,
who knows what I will do. As I sit on the couch the possibilities
are endless. I could be the next NFL star by 11am or win the
    Daytona 500.
The only thing I can't do today is lead a troop of soldiers on a Nazi
killing mission, at least not with my niece here with me.
This world is lucky I don't go outside because my mother was right:
I'm the i holding the w and n together in winner. I'm reminded of
    this right now,
as my PlayStation loads and I see the two 5 inch trophies
that my TV stand can hardly hold. I played tee ball for the Cubs, we
    didn't
finish first, second, or third in our league, but last. But it's not like
    we
were bad at baseball, we just didn't play well together. Too much
talent on one team can be a problem. I think they realized this and
    gave
us individual trophies for our talents. Johnny got his for being
able to sleep standing up and still play the game. Mark got his
for showing up to each game and pitching a few strike outs, but his
    dad
made him throw the trophy away, claiming everyone got one. And
    me,
I got mine for almost hitting a home run. I mean I could have made it
around all the bases if I was paying attention to the coach. But still
they realized my hitting ability. My niece asks to play Mario
    Brothers

so I load the game and start her on level 5-6. She burns through ten lives
in a matter of seconds, throws the controller to the ground and says she doesn't
want to play anymore. I tell her, she can never learn eye-hand coordination.
When she is older she will thank me for doing this to her.

Dear LadyFish,

Last night, after you went to bed,
I started thinking about what you

are doing to me. Here I am watching
tv night after night instead of studying

because you need the noise to fall asleep
and someone to watch over you

making sure you will be okay. But that doesn't
even work. Last night you needed another pill

to keep from checking your pulse every
two minutes. You agreed, you have no idea

what you're checking for but knew what
a raised pulse, and hurting arm felt like.

It's all in your head, I said, just go back to bed.
The pill finally kicked in giving me time

to pour our sodas down the sink and throw out
the burger and French fry wrappers. Can you

believe we had 56 cans of soda? I told you when
we got married I would do anything for you,

so I should be cooking you homemade meals
to keep you from having nightly anxiety attacks

Instead, I have to release the buildup of words
onto paper so I can sleep without being haunted.

Remodel

I watch my wife sitting at my desk,
stapling money order stubs to bill stubs.
She asks why we do it this way.
I tell her it is the only way I know how.
Putting each bill in its respective folder
and filing them away, she wants to know why
this is now her responsibility. It is better
if we both know how everything is done
around here, I say. But she is doing the bills
because she is innocent. My wife still
sees my mother as the woman who built
an add-on to her house without the help
of a husband or professional. The woman
who searched longshoremen for U.S. Customs
by herself in the middle of the night
while her partner sat in his squad car looking
at the dead end of an alley because he didn't
have the skills to back the car out.
But I don't just remember her this way
anymore. I remember the day I drove
from Reno to Fernley because it was the first
time my mother asked me for help. I sat
at the heart pine table she was unable to refinish
making a list of what bills needed to be paid,
wondering what a sternum eaten away by cancer
looked like, or a femur, or lungs, or why her body
created masses in delicate sections of her.
She took breaks between endorsing checks
telling me she was worn out and I was too.

HELEN SILVERSTEIN

Burn Pile

> *"Murder me God down in that basement,*
> *Murder my dreams so I stop wantin'."*
>
> *Caroline or Change*, Tony Kushner

She stood in the doorway considering his words, watching him back the Subaru down their long gravel driveway. He lowered the window, sticking his head out to yell one more time, "Put the damn thing on the burn pile."

Mary sat on the stoop, pulling her robe around her. It was spring, almost summer. But it felt like a fall morning, minus the frost on the yard. She studied the heavy dew drops each clinging to a blade of grass. Any heavier and surely they would drop onto the damp ground. She wondered what the tipping point would be.

She stepped down onto the grass, not caring that her pajama bottoms would soak up the dew. She called the dogs; they came tearing up from the field out back, swatting her with their tails, scrambling to get closest to her. There were three of them bumping against her legs, pushing their snouts into her hands. Mary knelt down, letting the dogs lick her face, burrowing her head in the fur of the oldest and the tallest-- a Shepherd mix, getting on in years, but still retaining his place as leader of the pack.

Mary allowed herself a moment to cry. Over a damned table, she chided herself, getting to her feet. The burn pile was around the side of the house. She wanted to have a look at it.

She stood with her dogs contemplating the pile. It sat about fifty yards from the house. Mary figured she could drag the table out here a piece at a time. But it wouldn't do her knee or her back any good. And he knew that.

She was a big woman, nearly six feet tall and strong, even if she had gone to fat in the usual places. That's what he'd be thinking: She can handle it; she's an ox of a woman. That was one of the names she'd heard in the course of their relationship, one of the many names that stuck. She had a catalogue of these tattoo names. Who's gonna want your fat ass anyway? Mary imagined him saying these words now as he drove to work, leaving her behind with his orders. Put it on the burn pile. She hated taking orders.

Standing here soaking wet won't get the job done, Mary thought. She turned away from the burn pile, heading to the house with the big dog leading the way, the little one nosing at her heels, and the middle one off again on a chase. She entered the house through the back door and toweled off Shep and Chico, getting the better part of the mud off them. Whistling at the door, she called the middle one, Gus, who did not respond. He'd come around later.

Mary stripped off her robe and wet pajamas, roughly drying off. Wrapped in a towel, she walked through the kitchen, set the kettle on low, and moved quickly through the dining room. She kept her eyes focused on the bay window they had installed. Below it, on the deep red and gold oriental carpet, lay the two ends of the table. She did not want to look. She latched the dog gate behind her, at the base of the stairs, where the house opened out into the TV room. The dogs weren't allowed upstairs, as they were when Mary lived alone. A compromise she was willing to make. The wood stove in the kitchen kept the downstairs comfortably warm. The dogs flopped down on the beds strewn around the stove, content.

Mary climbed the stairs to their bedroom. The old debate started in her head. Why did she stay with him? She had already put in six years trying, for one thing. And she wasn't getting any younger. She remembered well the long, dry spell that preceded this relationship. Did she want to end up alone? He fought dirty, yes, but he never hit her. And things did not go badly between them all the time. There was that. The good times. Like when he surprised her with the antique white cabinet for their master bathroom. She loved it, with its chipped paint showing through to yet an older color, pale green. It had a hand-towel rod underneath and she had opened the door to find three slender, scalloped shelves. A lady's cupboard: impractical, beautiful. He said it was for her potions, the name he gave to her collection of creams and lotions for her face. An indulgence, these potions, yet he had understood their importance to her, giving them a love name and the cupboard. Upstairs now, Mary peeked into the bathroom to look at the cupboard, still beautiful, still whole.

Yes, she reasoned, as she walked to the bed, the fact was that allowances had to be made. She decided to lie down for a minute, to think, to get this right in her head. No one was perfect. The winters were long here, isolated. Alcohol made its way into dark nights. Fuses shortened. No couple made it through winter unscathed, Mary was sure of it. But she could not tell her friends about their fights. About the names. The vulgar names he called her: cunt, f'ing slut. She was sure her friends would be appalled, would hate him for it, and would think less of her for putting up with it. Mary suspected there was a weight to this secrecy that kept her bound to him, a kind of complicity that she would allow such a thing.

Focus. She needed to focus on the good times. Nights watching movies together, a bowl of popcorn shared—simple pleasures that she treasured. Deciding on a house together last year. How they both instantly loved this one. She recalled how she had her heart set on an oriental carpet for the dining room, how much fun they had looking for just the right one; when they found it, he insisted they splurge and get it—even though it was several hundred dollars more than they had agreed to spend. It was revolting to think that the table, now split in two, sat on that same carpet. Not the point, she told herself. The point was he had been generous. And no one was perfect. The fight, after all, was her fault. She had been tired, pulling an extra shift, and had come home to find him watching TV, enjoying a beer, not even having bothered to clean up after himself in the kitchen. She lost it. She grabbed the remote, turned off the TV, ordering him to clean up the kitchen. When he balked, she said she didn't expect to come home from an extra shift, twelve long hours, to find the house a mess. No one asked you to take that shift, he countered. She was infuriated. We need the money, she told him, and then she crossed the line. She saw the line and she crossed it. Somebody around here has to make some money, she had said, knowing full well it bothered him that she earned more than he did. He shot up out of his recliner and came at her. She ran through the dining room, pushing a chair over to block his way for a second while she took cover. She never expected he would pick that chair up and crash it down on the table.

Mary got up, dressing quickly. Sweatpants, a top and old sneakers. Thinking wasn't getting her anywhere she wanted to be. She should shower, but the kettle was whistling. And she'd likely need a shower later after she hauled the table out. She took the stairs slowly. Going down was harder on her knees. She could hear the crackling, the low note of osteoarthritis setting in. She was finding it more difficult than she would admit to anyone to keep up with her job as a nurse at the local hospital. On her feet all day, lifting and bending. A younger woman's job.

Back in the kitchen Mary made tea for herself, black tea sweet and milky. She picked up a chair lying on its side, pulling it over to the counter, where she sat to sip her tea. Now she looked at the table. It could be fixed, she thought. The break was clean enough. There had been a weakness in the wood there. If only he had thought to put a plank under it, just to give the slightly sloping middle some support. But this was his first time refinishing a table, and she had shied away from offering suggestions.

The table had been her great grandfather's originally, kept up at camp, where things tended to be rustic and any furnishings were of a practical nature. This particular piece had gone through several iterations, until it kept only the original oak tabletop. The table itself was a mystery, sitting on a pedestal so low not even a child could sit at it comfortably. What had its use been? Surely there had been one, or it would have been tossed long ago. After her grandfather passed, Mary salvaged the old table. She wanted it, for them, for the start of their new life as co-owners of their very own home. It provided a touch of the old, of her family heritage, to grace this new beginning, to place the two of them, almost husband and wife—partners—in the continuum of her family history. The work he put into it, refinishing the top, taking it off its oddly low pedestal and fashioning proper legs for it at a proper height, made it the centerpiece of the dining room, proudly placed in front of the bay window.

Mary got up to begin the process of moving the table. She examined the break again. It could be fixed. She was sure of it. She recognized the tone of voice in his order, but she had to cross him on this. She knew the hole in the house without this table would be huge. A new table wouldn't erase that hole. Had he thought about that?

She got the toolbox and took the legs off, setting them one by one under the bay window. She was working fast now, not bothering to put a pad under her knees. She would pay for that later. She lifted one half of the table, carrying it through the front door. She carried it a few feet, and then rested. It was solid oak, and even half a top was heavy. She rubbed her back, judging the strain. She could keep going. Slowly she made it to her car, opening the hatch with one hand. She summoned her will and hefted the thing into the back. Mary repeated the procedure with the second half of the table, noting a sharp protest from her lower back. He knew she had been through two surgeries for herniated discs. He could have done this lifting. But of course, he wouldn't have put the table in the car.

She glanced toward the burn pile again.

***

When he came home that night, he demanded to know what happened to the table. Mary kept her back to him, preparing supper. She didn't answer.

"It's not on the burn pile."

"No."

"Then where?"

"I told you it could be fixed."

"You took that thing to be fixed after I told you not to."

She didn't answer. It wasn't really a question anyway, she reasoned.

"You know it won't be the same."

She kept quiet.

"Whatever you bring back here will not be my table."

Ours, she thought. Our table.

Now he came close behind her and yelled.

"I told you it can't be fixed. I said put it on the burn pile."

Mary smelled whisky on his breath.

Slowly, she put down the vegetable peeler, set aside the bowl of carrots. She moved carefully, turning off the stove. She kept her eyes down and circled around him toward the cellar door, entering her refuge.

He yanked on the door. He knew she had set the wooden slide latch across. He would have to break the door to get in. She doubted he would break something two days in a row. And without a cellar door, the house couldn't be kept warm or free of whatever animals took up residence down there.

Then came the names.

Mary sat on the same box she occupied last night, after he slammed the chair against the table. He must have counted on the chair breaking, not the table he had put so much work into.

In her mind she watched herself carry the names one by one to the burn pile. She struck a match.

Finally, the yelling ceased.

She listened to him stomp around above her. The dogs were whining at the cellar door. She wanted them with her, but there wasn't time. There was never time. She heard him open the front door and shoo the dogs out.

He would eat something now, grabbing what he could from the fridge. She heard the slam of the door, the pop of the beer can, then his heavy tread up the stairs to their bedroom.

Mary waited, her feet restlessly kicking the dirt floor of the cellar, her body tightly coiled against this stillness; the hard hand of her mind—a flat iron—pressing steadily down, restraining her, urging her to calm down, to think. Don't do anything you'll regret.

Mary moved from her seat, paced the confined space of the basement, bowing her head under the low ceiling. Dirt puffed up around her ankles as she moved. She rubbed her arms, chilled. She thought of him, of the table—knew she was right. "Stubborn," she called him, in the safety of the cellar. Pig-headed bitch, her mind supplied his retort.

She raised her head, grazing the low ceiling, listening for the quiet that signaled he was asleep. Satisfied that he was, she climbed the basement stairs, allowing her imagination to unfold as she stood tall in the hallway, free of the cellar's low ceiling.

Her mind traveled rapidly, her thoughts bold. She imagined moving through the kitchen—taking her purse, her keys, and the tea canister full of cash from its hiding place—daring to open the door, to leave this house. Outside, she envisioned whistling softly for her dogs, opening the car door for them. She would take the long gravel driveway slowly, headlights off, squinting to find her way.

Inside the house, immobilized, she reeled her mind in with the warning: Don't do anything you'll regret. Her body felt heavy, stolid, and immovable. Her thoughts slowed; she felt caution return. She decided against calling for the dogs. Too much noise. She wouldn't risk it. They would have to spend the night outdoors.

She climbed the stairs to their bedroom branding herself with the name coward, adding this night to the others, times she almost left—her internal ledger bulging with guilt. She opened the door. He was lightly snoring

She undressed, sliding in next to him.

Her eyes closed, her racing mind still out there—on the road, free, waiting for a plan to take shape. But no plan came.

No plan. No house. No man.

Alone.

Shuddering, Mary edged closer to her almost-husband. Familiar, warm. He stirred, stretching his arm over her. The way he did. The way she liked. Her body began to relax.

She wanted this, needed this. No shame in that, she told herself. No.

What had she been thinking, defying him about a table? It was just a table, for heaven's sake. And starting two fights two days in a row? What was wrong with her? She'd end up alone, alright, if she continued down that road: He would leave her. But this could be fixed; she was sure of it.

She would call the repair man tomorrow. Tell him to get rid of the table. Put it on the burn pile for all I care, she thought, before sleep took her.

PEGGY AYLSWORTH

The Fathers

1.

What then, if you'd been Joyce, rubbing
your brains into Shakespeare, Aquinas,
to say nothing of Homer, Hebrew & metempsychosis,
walking the streets of Dublin,
minding more in one day in June
than most men glimmer in all their years?
I'd have run beside you
along the Liffey, the smells of
the marketplace, the pubs, even the puke
at the curbs, but more, I'd hear
the hum & murmur in your head
in the stretch of your stride. Your hand
would move this way & that & I'd know,
He's thinking of the Lady of the Bloomers,
the soft down between her thighs.
And then you'd speak of the isosyllabic
alliteration of the Welsh englyn,
render a few lines into English
in a Gaelic voice rising in its querying.
You would be a stout one in this world
too thin, leaving us (you, me, well, everyone)
embarrassed to bring a pot of warm beans to a neighbor,
never mind the poetry of Ezra Pound.

2.

Harder to forgive, the missing orchard,
the country house at Melikhovo & mostly you
at the new farming, "mountains
of cucumbers, amazing cabbages"; exhaustive
patient doctoring in the cholera epidemic; writing
(bushels of letters!) to Suvorin, plans to meet
in the Crimea to "write, talk, eat." Sitting near
the tile stove, drinking sweet tea, snow at the windows,
your quick, kind eyes an encyclopedia.
And to be heard by you! In the spring
together through the fields & you angry
at your hemorrhoids even as you praised
the novels of Pisemsky. To have you as my tutor!
No old regrets of wasted years before the books
took hold. Take me to task as you did
Shavrova, writing of S with little knowledge
(How ironic, *that* disease!). Would the forest
be alive with endless variety, never to bore
you, my tone of voice each day pitched to a different
bird? Or would I have laughed, enjoying your "ferocity"?

3.

I've always loved twilight, hanging
between. Does the day begin as you come
halfway through the door, the Hartford house
no more a haven than the purple light?
Everything you bring in the mid-point of your eye,
even where you've been, the Southern round,
moves toward me through that door. You've
forgotten the green & orange air, the screech
of peacocks till you hear me calling
my new name. To be your child, yet be
the moon, not the necessary idea, I sit

undeniably at the table with you, eating
figs & pineapple, saying No. You
with your in-turned ears hear nothing
negated. A bowl with elliptical leaves stretching
toward us forces me to see the red summer you
longed for. Sunday morning in the park we laugh,
your presence spinning mine to a blade of grass
grown higher than the trees,
despite restrictions against my questionable blood,
the insistent sound of bells.
When day reaches day, when sun reaches sun
you leave for *the little island of geese and stars*.

Song for Women at a Hard Time

It's Friday evening in L.A.
Five women talk,
frank as the fish, the cheese.
In the room Zuni pottery,
paintings, the work of weavers.
We eat the bread we no longer bake.
Our hair is whiter now but not quite honest.
Something needed at the root of loss.
Fathers of our children shift
to other lives or none.

We tend ourselves and those still
licking soles of damaged feet,
remember stone-age streets,
careful in dark alleys, cherishing
rooms like this where at dusk
we speak to one another
while cars below pause at the signs
and pull away.

How It Was, 1935

Orphaned, I was rescued
by my wealthy aunt and uncle.
He had built a house for her in Newark,
Mediterranean and high terraced.
I moved in.
She learned of loss and profit
reading tiny figures
in the daily paper,
pleased with reports
from children
safe at Vassar, Princeton.

Suddenly, the crash.

The wipe-out forced us
to New York, a fifth floor walk-up,
might have been
just one more change of rooms,
except for nightly roaches.
Crumbs clinging to his vest,
my uncle, bowed,
had lost his prayer,
his thunder thinned to gray,
as he waited for events
that had already happened.
In the yellow kitchen light
enameled porcelain table
with its corner nicked to black,
my tongue took refuge as I ate

the buttered rye, my secret taste....
slightly sour, rough with caraway.
I looked at the moon
as they complained of Roosevelt
and his socialist ideas.
After supper, soapy water
puckered my fingers.
In the living room they gathered
at the radio and listened
to Jack Benny. I never
heard them laugh out loud.

KAREN ENGLISH

Moonrise

Ma Blanche heard Cap before she saw him. He was out there
shuffling his feet on the fine gravel of her freshly swept yard.
Messing up the neat ridges left by her broom. Ah well, nothing lasted
forever. She knew he'd come to plead his father's case and was just
working up the nerve to climb the steps, rattle the screen, and shield
his eyes against it to see what he could see. She set the iron down on
the board propped on two chairs and went to the door.

"Watcha want?"

"Hey, Ma Blanche." He was shirtless and wearing a pair of his
father's overalls. They drooped off the shoulders, still too big. He'd
cuffed them so they wouldn't drag. Now, he stood there with his
arms hanging at his sides.

She stepped out onto the porch and crossed her arms—peeved at
this interruption in her work. She had seven shirts to starch and iron
for Mrs. Markam over in Repton and sheets and pillow cases yet to
wash, dry, and iron by evening. What did this boy want with her on
this day?

"Papa wants to know if you comin' to the field tonight. The
moon's gonna be out and they gonna to be workin' down there in
Ol' Phelps's field probably til' midnight. Papa needs you to help him
catch up."

"He knows I ain't gonna to do that. I already told him. I don't
know why he sent you over here, tryin' to soften me up. Ain't gonna
do no good." She looked off toward the stand of pine, then up at the
long loose clouds drifting in the August sky. Heat seemed to rise off
the hard packed red dirt road that ran past her place.

"He wants to know if you can come this once." Cap raised his pleading eyes to her and she thought the boy just might start crying. He was too damn sensitive. She feared he was going to have a hard row to hoe in this life.

"Go on. I got work to do. Anyway, your papa know what I told him," she said but in a quieter voice that let them both know her resolve might not be ironclad.

Cap's gaze had dropped to the ground at his feet as if he were trying to hide from her his small pinch of hope.

"Get on now and leave me be."

He turned on his heels but she thought she detected a bounce in his step.

It wasn't fair this request Blair—Cap's father, *her* husband, was making. He was a good man. She knew that and they had a pretty good arrangement, she staying in her place and he staying in his. It was their own way of being married and she didn't care if people understood it or not. It was their way—both having lost their own spouses within a year of each other. She was childless but Blair had had a bunch of kids. All grown—except Cap, who was fifteen.

Three had gone up to Mobile, two farther north all the way up to Chicago.

A couple of them promptly forgot they had a daddy. The others did what they could, sent money from time to time. And, that helped.

She wasn't gonna do it. Blair's situation was hopeless. He could work day and night. He wasn't ever gonna catch up. Phelps would see to that. What had he told Blair when Blair had brought his cotton to be weighed? What did Mr. Phelps say?

"Dang, Blair, if it'd only been one more bale—then we'd be square."

Hadn't she wanted to sink right into the earth and have it swallow her up then and there watchin' her husband walking away, defeated? Later Blair had sat on her steps a long time with his eyes on the moon rising over a bank of night clouds figurin' and figurin'. He wasn't ever gonna be square with Phelps. He could count on that.

She looked out her kitchen window across the open field. Wasn't that a lovely moon brightening up the night sky? Look how it hung low and big above that field that separated her place from Phelps's cotton field. Someone was singing, "Sweet By and By" as sweetly as the perch-coo of the mourning dove seeking its mate. Oh—it was about to draw her. It was about to make her tie that red bandana on her head, take down the croker sack from the nail on the wall by the door.

And, that's just what she did. She tied the bandana around her head, got her croker sack down from its nail and stepped out onto the porch and felt just a whisper of a breeze in the settled heat. She had to help Blair make beyond his quota. Mr. Phelps was paying $1.00 per hundred pounds. She had to help him have some hope of clearing up his debt and getting a little bit ahead.

The week before, still feeling the sting of that man cheating Blair, she'd run into him in town in front of the feed store.

"Blanche, where you been? I need to get my crop to the gin before the price falls. I could sure use you."

Looking down all the while she said, "Sorry, Mr. Phelps. I got me another job." It was only a tiny white lie. But actually it wasn't no lie. Washing and ironing *was* another job. One she'd much rather do than step foot in his cotton field.

Now she counted twenty bent backs at least. Look at them poor souls, she was thinking to herself, when one stood up to empty his sack in the basket at the end of the row, then climb in to stomp the cotton down. Blair. She wasn't ready to join him, just yet. She wanted to look at him for a bit.

He had his own little patch. Ten good acres of his own land that he'd been working. Between that and Mr. Phelps, she thought, poor Blair didn't ever stop workin'. But still he owed. He owed for the fertilizer and the cotton seed and the month's supply of groceries from Phelps's store. All that went in Phelps's book and everything had to be settled up before anybody could clear a profit from their own land. Picking day and night... That was the only way.

She watched her husband wipe the sweat from his brow with the back of his hand. There was a kind of quiet energy in the way he was starting for that next row. The man had hope. All those bent backs dragging those long sacks behind them, had hope. She watched them a while, then she slipped the strap of her own sack over her head and went on down to join them.

JENNY ROSSI

Let's Go to Arizona

People talk about heat and say things like, "hot enough to fry an egg on the sidewalk" or "like a blow-dryer on high. In your face."

Closer to the truth, it's hot enough to sauté the elderly in their homes. The ones too poor to fix the AC. Christ, it's only on the news every other night. Along with some moron who tossed a puppy out a car window, doing 95 on the freeway. I don't mind watching the news when I can, because I find out what's going on a few blocks away. Robbery, assault. Booooring. Remote clicks. Oooh, another puppy out the window. Shooting. I only have five channels to flip through, but it is the spice of my life.

So that's what I think when I walk from work in Phoenix. I could be frying to death in my home, 80 years old. Instead, I'm a healthy 18, frying to death on 36th and Van Buren. After three years, I don't know how to use the bus system, though it's cheap and the grab-ass by alcoholic perverts is free. I just can't bring myself to do it. Homeless people ride the bus all day. I'd rather pretend my car broke down, and I'm walking home from work with that stubborn, helpless pride of the working class.

A car slows down. "Babe, you need a ride?"

"Nah. I'm almost there," "there" being the mythical place were sex offenders don't offer car rides. I'm actually far away from wherever "there" is. I don't turn my head or stop.

"I know you do. I see you walking every day."

The car is purring along happily to keep pace with my quick walk. Cars are honking at him. Probably thinking I'm an angry girlfriend.

"Listen" he continues, "Just get in. I know you need a ride. I can drop you off wherever you want." Like a ditch, a dumpster, or chopped up in his fucking freezer.

I slow down. I really get a look at this guy. I kind of want to see who's trying to abduct me. Morbid curiosity.

He's like, my age. Nice. Good to know my generation is really moving up. I'm so relieved now. Faith in the world restored.

Some more cars honk. Most speed past. I walk faster. And faster. It seems to be some kind of cue. He speeds up. Panic worms through my chest. I'm sweating from adrenaline now. "Hey, I'm a good guy, I see you walking every day, I always watch you when I drive past. You need a ride." I shake my head "no" tersely.

I'm about to walk up to a random house, pretend I live there, and ask to use the phone. I don't have anyone to call, but he'd be gone by the time I got out. Too bad many doors don't open to strangers in the part of town tiny, blonde white girls aren't supposed to live.

He starts yelling. Asking if I think I'm too good to take a ride. (I don't want to point out that, yes, I do think so. I could have taken the bus.)

Right on cue, a van pulls up behind him.

Of course. A van. Like to stash my struggling body in. Duh.

Everything freezes. I'm mid-step to bolting through a rock garden yard littered with dog poo, leading to a small rundown house with iron grate windows. At that moment I hear a loud, brassy voice yell, "HEY."

The guy in the car looks really confused.

Everyone pretty much stops. I see a fat, tan man in a wife-beater. The van door is haltingly slid open. By a little girl. Fat man rumbles low to me, "You know that guy, honey?"

I shake my head frantically. I wonder why people who want to kill me call me pet names first. God, what a sick world. Then I really notice the little girl sitting in the back. She looks unharmed. Her mouth opens to "Daddy, why are we stopping?"

He doesn't answer. He cranes his neck out the window. "HEY, THIS GIRL DON'T WANNA RIDE, GET THAT?" followed up with "I JUST CALLED THE COPS." Oh, great. Perfect if we need help three hours from now. Cops are useless over here.

The car speeds off. I get the feeling I really shouldn't be taking rides today. I see the fat man scribbling on a paper, and turns to me. "Young lady, you need a ride?"

Yes. I do. I don't care if you're crazy, and you kidnapped that little girl to lure young women into accepting rides, I tell the man mentally. In fact, that's a very good idea. I'd use it myself if I were in the abducting business. Applauding his good sense, I climb in the van. The little girl just stares.

"Now, sweetheart, I saw you kept shaking your head and walking, do you have a cell phone?"

Nope, So you can commence with the torture now.

"Um, my roommate has one."

Fat Man snorts, "You really shouldn't be out here without a phone. It's a bad area. Now, my wife's a dispatch, and I took the guy's license plate down. You go on and call it in, okay?"

I nod. While I give him the cross streets that I live on, the little girl babbles away happily. When he pulls up to the apartment, he stops the van. "Now listen, I got some mace on my key ring. It ain't much, but it's more than what you got now."

I take it with fumbling fingers, red-faced by more unexpected kindness as he shows me how to use it, though I am fully literate and could read the directions. I try to mumble my thanks, but he's impatient to go.

Grasping the license plate number on paper, I slide out of the car regretfully, wishing I could trade places with his little girl. I have also left a little of my pride and self-reliance sticking to the seats with my damp sweat, nothing Fat Man would notice. Walking into the apartment, I throw the paper in the trash and sit down on our Rent-a-Center couch to watch the news.

NINA RUBINSTEIN ALONSO

Things: Yard-Sale Karma

Strangers turn things over
check sets for missing pieces
squint at a brass frame
with the photo torn out

no one wants that black vase
dusty years on the shelf
but a girl buys the bracelet
I can't wear any more

because he gave it to me
pain leaves scars silent
scratches no polish can clean
no magic scare away

now spring rain sprinkles
the green wheelbarrow
my daughter pushed at four
time to drag things inside

first those canvas beach chairs
dismal as the ex that chose them
but a small blond woman
points and offers cash

so I smile with queenly calm and say
'it's a deal' surprised she doesn't
see stains of bad karma
which I guess belong only to me.

E. A. FOW

A Collection of Crashes

Looking back, there were several moments during which Angie could have waited a minute longer or moved forward another inch or two. At any of those explicit points in time, the accident could have been avoided, and thus never have existed or even been imagined. However, an extra minute or inch forward or back could have inflated the situation or even triggered catastrophe. She had had a lucky life, but it was the kind of luck that is best appreciated in retrospect.

The first accident of note was when she broke her wrist while roller-skating at the age of eight. She and Carolyn Smith crashed into each other; Angie fell backwards. It seemed to take forever to hit the ground, so she had time enough to stretch her hands out to catch herself, and when she finally hit, it was with such force that she snapped her wrist. She was lucky; if she had fallen forward, like Carolyn did, she would have gone face first into the concrete. She, too, would have ruined her nose and mouth and would have suffered Carolyn's lifelong hesitance to kiss.

When she was fourteen, she woke up uneasy and surrounded by smoke. She opened her eyes, unsure if the small lights dancing at the edge of her sheet were actually there. The air smelled strange, and then she knew: everything was on fire. She was panicked but strangely also felt clarity. She couldn't hear anything, but she knew what she had to do, leaping from her bed on a mission to stop the fire from spreading. She found just the bedding was alight, beat at it with her arms, then gathered it up and ran through the house to the bathroom where she threw it all into the bathtub and turned on the water to douse it. She was so focused that she didn't feel her foot crash into the doorjamb of the bathroom and was unaware of her four stubbed toes. The room filled with the smell of wet, burned fabric and averted danger, and only then did she get scared. She patted herself down, looking for burns or any evidence that she'd just carried fire from one end of the house to the other, but there was nothing. She sat down on the toilet and looked at the wet mess in the bathtub. Why wasn't she burned? What if she hadn't woken up at all? What if she had died in her sleep, cooked to death? Why did her feet hurt? She looked down expecting to see charred flesh; instead, she saw the ragged ends of her stubbed toes, blood welling. She suddenly felt sick. She didn't know whether to wake up her mother or not, and she chose not. Stumbling back to her room, she discovered the source of the original problem; her bedside lamp had fallen from the dresser into the drawer of t-shirts below. She lay on her sheetless bed with nothing to pull over her, her feet throbbing, and realized there was no good reason she was still alive.

When she was twenty-three, she was hit by a car. Her boyfriend called out to her, lunged forward to grab her, to pull her back to the safety of the footpath, but both she and the car were too fast. It swung around the corner and lifted her off the ground. She buckled and then was flipped up and onto the bonnet. She spun around and slid back down to the ground so quickly that she could see the grill of the car still advancing toward her. This is it, she thought: I'm going to die. She wasn't afraid, just clear. Then it stopped... inches from her face. She was crouched down like a frog, and David was looking at her, paralyzed. He should have run out to her, but he couldn't and just stood there; he thought she was broken, that she was torn and fractured under her coat and wondered what he was supposed to do with the pieces. But then she popped up with such force that she bounced. He couldn't see the look on her face, imagining it was anguish, pain, not the huge smile that would confront him when she turned around. The driver of the car took her elbow. Are you all right? Do you need to go to the hospital? I can take you. We were just there—I know the way. Are you all right? Oh my God, I'm so sorry!

She was all right, completely all right, and felt very sorry for the father who had hit her with his car while bringing his child home from the emergency room. She looked into the car where his tired, anxious wife was sitting, and she looked through to the back where the little girl with a hospital eye patch sat in her car seat. David finally put his arm around her, and she wondered where he'd been. When they went home to her apartment afterward, and David wouldn't stop talking about how terrible it was to have to watch her be hit by a car, the shock spread through her. When he finally stopped talking and asked if she could make him a cup of coffee while he sat down because he was feeling shaky, she realized it was time to get a new boyfriend.

When Angie woke in the morning he was, unfortunately, still there and oblivious that she was sore and stiff from the impact and the aftermath; he still needed comforting. She wondered why she was still alive, why these things kept happening to her and were always almost (but never quite) terrible. Life was too random to even feel grateful, but she certainly felt relieved.

She didn't get rid of her boyfriend until she crashed to the ground again three weeks later, the victim of her own stylish shoe and uneven ground. This time he didn't even notice she'd gone down. She lay on the concrete, her face flat against it, winded and aware that she was going to bleed, probably from her knees, possibly from the side of her face, definitely from her hands which had skated along instead of stopping the fall. Eventually she lifted her head and saw he was walking further and further away, still talking on his phone. Someone offered her a hand, asked her if she was okay, kindly smoothed her dress down as she struggled up, and commented anxiously on the welling blood. She wondered, briefly, if perhaps there was reason to everything after all.

Five years later she sat in her car on Peachgrove Road, stuck behind a truck that had suddenly stopped moving. Her dog sat in the passenger seat, tongue hanging out, panting hard, delirious that he was along for the ride. Her baby made soft noises in her sleep in the car seat behind. Angie wanted to look at her in the rear vision mirror but knew she had to watch the truck. Because she was watching, she saw the backing lights flick on. She heard the beep beep beep, so she put her own car into reverse and backed, and hit the car that was too close behind her. She looked in the mirror and saw the car she'd just hit, and a car behind it, and another beyond it, and another, and another. She looked forward to the truck and started slamming her hand up and down on the horn, but the truck kept coming, so she kept trying to back up, hoping the car behind her would suddenly do the same, but the car never moved, and the truck kept coming. It was a delivery truck, the kind with a high loading gate that could be unfolded into a ramp, which was now poised to come through the windscreen at exactly the same height as her head. She stopped ramming the horn and didn't scream, not wanting to wake and scare her baby or panic the dog. All she could do was keep her foot on the accelerator, trying to push the car behind her. Finally she was reversing, an inch, then maybe two, but the truck was reversing more quickly. She couldn't quite believe it wasn't going to stop, that the metal gate was going to come through the windscreen. The dog jumped down off the seat and hid under the glove compartment. She took his hint and turned and ducked down, crawling between the seats to unbuckle her baby. She heard the crunch of the truck against her car, then the gate spiked through the window, which buckled and twisted around it. She heard metal scraping on metal and the continuing cracking of the glass. The truck was coming through the window at them, slow and inevitable. She didn't feel clear this time, she felt driven by wave upon wave of fear for her daughter, and enormous regret. She got the baby out of the seat, but there was no time to go anywhere; she couldn't get out of the car or even get into the back seat, so she pulled her baby under her, pressing down as low between the seats as she could without hurting her child. She could hear her dog panting, just as happy as he had been before, but she wasn't sure where he was. Her baby gurgled in delight under her and began burrowing, fussing around looking for a breast. Angie tensed her whole body, determined the truck wouldn't get through her, and then it all stopped. It was strangely quiet. She turned her head - the gate was still inside her car, the tip of it right above her, but it was no longer moving. She breathed and noticed how loud it sounded. Then the crunching started again and she cried out, but death did not come for them because everything was moving in the opposite direction: the glass buckled outward, wrapped obscenely around the metal, then pieces of it fell outwards into the air, and then the truck was gone, disconnected, and then it was further and further away, and she realized the truck was driving off. It had just driven backwards then forwards through her car, and now its driver was running away.

She clambered back into her seat, breathing hard. She didn't know what to do; she wanted to chase the truck down and to punch her fist through the face of the driver, but writing down the license plate was probably more realistic, so while balancing her baby on her lap with one arm she did that. She helped her dog back up onto the seat and put her head on the steering wheel. She thought she would cry, but instead she just shook, impotent, relieved, angry. Her baby cooed.

When the police arrived, she handed over the number and the name to the officer. When she and the baby and the dog got home, she reported the accident to the insurance company, and handed over the number and name to them, too. Her husband said it would just be a matter of time, but nothing happened, no one contacted her, nothing happened. The police and insurance company knew the truck had committed a hit and run on a car full of a woman, a dog, and a baby, and apparently it wasn't necessary to do anything about it. The insurance paid out, so no one was interested in pursuing it further.

Angie wondered if she was supposed to be grateful: grateful she hadn't ruined her face, grateful she hadn't burned up her skin or disappeared in fiery sleep without even knowing it, grateful she bounced off the car, grateful the truck hadn't killed any of them. She did feel relieved, but she knew she wasn't grateful; she was perturbed about what else a bright, sunny day could bring for no good reason and which way her life would turn.

BEAR JACK GEBHARDT

Old Friends, Parting

Once before, as young men,
we two old friends parted—him
stuck with truck stop coffee and donuts—
me saying, "I'll go on, you follow."
we'd learned the hard way
two thumbin's harder
than one.

We made plans exactly where we'd meet
on the Cape after the sun went down,
planned to maybe make a drift wood fire,
drink rum, celebrate, dance and sing.

"Meantime," I said, "take care, friend.
See you soon, hopefully, down the road."
I pointed my thumb, back then,
towards the far galaxies
shining bright and beautiful
under the distant overpass.

And now we're old men together.
We did meet up at the shore. We did laugh,
sing, celebrate. Since then, lots of tides
have come and gone.
"You go on," I tell him now.
I reach for his hand, his big thumb
caresses mine. He's the one
going ahead, hooked to the monitors
in this god forsaken distant place.
"We'll meet again, bro, we'll celebrate,"

I tell him, "laugh, sing, drink rum,
if they have it there on the distant shore."

"If they don't," he says. "I'm not going."

I walk from his hospital room,
The weak light
of his heart monitor flashing
the distant galaxies.

After my tears,
in the basement cafeteria
I wait, speak softly with his sister
over coffee and donuts.

Faces of Fast Friends

As a kid I observed a space—two, three
inches at most, between my outer face
and the inner me. I asked my buddy
Glenn, "you feel that space, too—outside to in,
two, three inches?" He said no, he didn't,
didn't know what inner gap I was pointing to.

The space narrowed, grew less as I became
more accustomed to my body. Friend Glenn,
a fast learner, was undoubtedly stuck
identity-wise, into his body
at the time I asked about the face gap.

Then I learned about girls, started feeling
my own magnificent juices rising,
so the gap between inner and outer
thinned and soon, me and my raging hormones
were one. I was my physical body,
like everybody else was their body
and it was body to body contact,
excitements that kept my attention locked
(in the body) decade after decade.

Now as a mature guy with silver hair,
having had lots of fun with this body
(and hers!) I find the childhood space again
appearing... a point, here inside my skull,
two, three inches behind my wrinkled face,
where I AM—where attention, awareness
reality is. This body's movement
is incidental, not necessary,
secondary to the real me who's here.

Here in my maturity, however,
this "I am" that I am, two, three inches
inside the frail skull bone, is infinite—
more than infinite: it's wordless, spaceless,
timeless, formless—this face can come and go,
be first young, then grow old— it has nothing
whatsoever to do with the timeless
attention, awareness, being I am,
space-like, in which all things, the galaxies,
the universes, all forms rise and fall.

"You feel what's just inside, behind your face?"
I'd ask Glenn again, if he were here.
He's a fast learner. Probably by now
he'd reply, "Oh sure. The face I'm wearing
now is the face I was wearing before
my parents were born." I'd nod my old head.
"I can dig it," I'd agree. Being fast
friends since childhood, we're able to talk
about almost anything in the world.

BILL DILL

Encounter on the Charles

By chocolate brambles on the bank two geese,
black heads fixed like mine mid-stream –
a straight and fading line of froth,
stirred by a seeker,
standing on a narrow board
and paddling east.

I'm years past changing places,
moving fast like him,
a hurried Sunday driver
scanning more, but seeing less.

Not the fragile sprigs of horsetail,
violets in the grass,
clumps of pungent cress –
whispers of spring
the geese and I have found.

She's Ivy Now

At the stone shop looking
so alone, a woman a third my age
asks to have a flask of greens
to sort while I probe other jars
for size and shape, not hues,
to fill a copper ring my lover
prizes not for provenance
but fit to her arthritic hand.

"How are you, Mary?" the owner asks.
"I'm not Mary any more – I'm Ivy now –
the judge said yes last week – the new me
is life and love. I'm saving $500 to add
the tattoo I've drawn to climb my back
from hips to hairline, with room for wreaths
when passions flower and triumphs come."

A different way to log a life! – for what
my lover's diamond cost, sixty years ago.
Memories are *our* tattoo; twice lost,
twice found, our gem was finally tossed
by a wire bridge's ragged mesh to roil with
other rocks in a raging mountain stream.

As Ivy fingers idly with her pile, I find
two stones that fit and flit some light
like real jewels. Eight bucks buy both.
My wife will choose, then we'll boast a
new and frugal way to advertise our vows.

"Good luck," the owner sighs as Ivy leaves,
and again to me – "to mate a ring and stone,"
she says, "there is no everlasting glue."

Juleigh Howard-Hobson

Crap

It had been a long year. A long couple of years. Decades, even. Was it really decades? Yeah. Decades. Which was a depressing thought in and of itself.

Decades. I had wasted decades working in shitty little independent bookstores, doing nothing in particular with myself except grow disgusted with humanity in general and my co-workers in particular.

Nice.

So here I was. Walking out to my car in middle of the day. Leaving my register. Leaving my freaking register. Was I crazy? No. Yes. Maybe. But no more crazy than I was this morning when I was actually still working behind the register of the shitty independent bookstore that I hated with all my guts.

Now I was free. I had options again.

I could move back with my folks. Or, whatever it is you call a divorced parent—a folk? I had two of them. Either one was as good —or as bad—as the other one. They both thought I had wasted my life being a fuck off, and while both of them pretty much tolerated me okay, they didn't really enjoy me. Which was fair enough, really. I was a fuck off. But I did prefer to be enjoyed than tolerated. It would be infinitely better to remain at my own place as long as I could.

Which was exactly how long? I had a little over three weeks left before rent was due, and after that the landlord couldn't kick me out until about three more months had passed, so I was cool there. I had the summer. Food would be a hassle, sure, and bills. But I could sell some of the books I'd swiped over the years. The irony would be good for my soul, if not for my personal library.

My car ran alright. Well, as alright as a 1985 Ford Crown Victoria was ever going to run. I used to dig its wine colored funky out-of-style squareness; now I just dug its untheftworthiness and the fact that it still ran.

We all make compromises as we grow older.

I opened the car door. It squeaked, and the window rattled around like a free floating wall of glass stuck in a ... a what? I don't know. A big square flat can or something. I was not in the mood to make artistic comparisons.

I sat down on the big burgundy-colored vinyl bench seat, the door still open, one foot still on the ground. Did I dare? Did I dare to do this? Leave my job? Say fuck it and slam my door and start the engine on a whole new chapter of my life?

Well.

Well.

Well, well, well.

I sat there. Stared out of the window. Thought about my folk and folk. About my rent. About my landlord. About the price of gas. About the fact that I needed to finish some tattoo work on my arm. About the fact that I liked food. About the fact that I knew there was no better place for a fuck off like me to work in than a shitty independent bookstore like this one.

Not that I liked that. I just knew it.

I thought about life, death, hamburgers, movies, future prospects, lunch dates, and hair cuts. All those things that I knew cost money. I thought about money. I thought about how I didn't have any. I thought about how I could—in all reality—just go back into the book store and say nothing about any of this. It wasn't like I announced that I quit. I simply left.

I bit my lip. I looked up at the sky through my dirty and rock-chipped windshield. I knew what I was going to do. I didn't like it though. I just knew I was going to do it. I was going to drive away. Be a fuck up. Again.

Then this thing happened.

A bird crapped right on the windshield, right in my field of vision. Right when I was looking dramatically up into the sky, thinking about all the things I was going to miss out on in life if I continued being a fuck off.

Splat.

It occurred to me that it was meaningless. The bird had no idea where its crap was going to land. It was just crap. Random crap.

I moved the foot that was still outside the car into the car, then I pulled the door shut. The glass rattled, but it didn't fall out.

I put the key in the ignition and turned it on to "accessories." The wipers sprang to life, smearing bird crap back and forth.

I turned them off. Then I got out of the car and went back in to work.

ACE BOGGESS

**Letter to Kids on Bicycles Screaming Playfully
Outside My Window on a Sunday Morning**

Spring is no Cathedral, sunlit tarmac
not a haloed likeness burned in brilliant glass.
I forgive you for intruding
on my quiet hour, forcing me
to see again the Aprils of childhood.
Your shrill, knifing cries that sing delight
were lost amidst a timid youth spent alone
as though in a confessional waiting
on the priest that never comes.
Yet Springtime is no chapel of pews
to silence you— this rebellion
the one true passion play: spiritual,
Holy. You minister to me the Gospel
of Sunlight, chapter & verse. I listen.

Possible Side Effects

alprazolam (Xanax) numbs burdens & what pizzazz
blue skies brightly bluster dulling even distance between say
cocaine & codeine so different in nature yet how they tax
darkness then lead to darkness in the soulless hollow
end you can swallow snort smoke shoot an IV
fluid drip until you yourself drip into fluid or burn with flu
God can't make up his mind between pleasure pain & whatnot
Heroin for example the big H is so like kissing a mermaid on her fishy lips as the tide's mean roar
jags at you knifelike & powerful slashing the EQ
killing the woofers & tweeters in your head pop pop pop
loud as caged-baboon screechings at the Pittsburgh Zoo
methadone helps softly refocusing the opiate lens within
now that you're trying to stop trying to get away from
Oxycontin siren songs with their constant heavenly pull
pulling pulling toward the next hell the next kick
"Quit" your friends tell you "Put it down" as if a glass of OJ
right nothing's that easy with benzos goofballs junk booze I
shit you not Iranian revolutionaries overthrowing the Shah
took less time & effort to place their hated pig
under the ax & we haven't even touched on crack or crank if
Vicodins & Valiums won't do the two small C's release
wickedness within enough to make you wish you were dead
Xed out shuffled off this mortal coil tracing the end of your arc
yes you've run out of options now a mindless blob
zero chance you'll ever be a good son to your mama

CHARLES LEGGETT

Love TV in the "Love Tent"

Installation, Adelaide Arts Festival, 2002

Surreal admixture of Reality
TV and the anticlimax in *The Wizard*
of Oz about not paying any mind
to the man behind the curtain. Folks were sitting
on couches, or on cushions, drinks in hand;
the tent was sporting its own bar (no Irish).

What people watched, upon a large-screen (closed
circuit) television: interviews
with twenty-something single folk or couples,
conducted either with a cavalier
irreverence or giddy, cloying candor,
regarding their amours, such as they were.

The interviews completed, out the subjects
stumbled, grinning, bleary-eyed from bright
lights that emanated from—well, from *behind*
the curtain. Yes. They did the interviews
behind a scheme of hanging arrases,
a tent-within-a-tent—and right behind

the frigging television we all watched!
Who needs a *satellite* or tv *station*?
Bring cameras, serve some drinks and call it "Love"!

CATHY BRYANT

Broken Biscuits

She'd bring home great heavy boxes
of broken biscuits she'd got cheap;
in each box, one or two unblemished circles
or unchipped wafers—unlicensed perfection
that had crept in.

These prizes rounded our eyes with excitement:
the joy of *extra*, of *not supposed to happen*.
So much more delicious than ordinary biscuits,
whose flawlessness was merely expected uniformity.

Mum tried to appear unbroken, could conjure
appearances out of anything, out of nothing.
We believed in her intactness until
we grew too old for biscuits,
brushing the crumbs from our faces.

But we saw her crumbled too often,
fallen on tables, soggy at the edges,
dunked in too much gin. It took time
to realise that the biscuits weren't really that heavy
—that wasn't why she staggered.

We'd put the kettle on then, and sit her down,
try to comfort with a cup of tea, and the familiar
shape and sweetness of an Oreo or graham cracker
pressed gently, hopefully, into her palm.

The Clothes of Heavy Trouble

Peeling them off
—the heavy coats of responsibility,
the clinging underthings of guilt,
clammy and hidden in their shame;
the itchy top of stress,
the tight shoes of fear,
the pinching collar of tasks,
the digging waistband of obligation

—she tries to replace them with herbal teas,
meditation, window open or closed,
whale songs, breathing exercises
and all in relaxed nudity.
But the clothes lie in wait.
She can see them from her bed:
arms, legs, collars all slithery
and poised to pounce if she gets up.
Herbal tea won't stop 'em
pulling her down again in the morning,
and on top of it all,
the washing needs doing.

Skimming Moments

Mummy, where do ripples come from?

From the stone pushing the water, darling.

And where do the ripples go when they stop?
And where did I come from?

You remember then that because of the most
extraordinary concatenation of circumstances
you looked up and he looked up and your hearts
gave a lurch and somewhere a butterfly flapped
its wings like a beating heart and that's
how typhoons start and children get born.

You squeeze your daughter's hand and wonder
how to explain chance, love, biology, mathematics,
loss. You smile helplessly, sadly at her
and she laughs back and dances

BRANDON FRENCH

Tall

1.

For as long as she could remember, Tookie Basch wanted to be tall, like one of those willowy teenagers with legs and necks like giraffes in *Vogue* and *Mademoiselle*. And one Monday morning in April, after a long night of vodka martinis and shameless flirtation with the keyboard player in the band at her married sister's 40th birthday party, Tookie woke up seven feet tall.

She was, admittedly, very hung over but that could not account for why the blond oak floor was two extra feet from her eyes when she looked down. Or that her feet would no longer fit into her Fuzzy Froggy bedroom slippers.

She walked barefoot to the full length mirror across from the bed but she could only see herself from the waist down. She had to move backwards, banging her head as she passed through the doorway into the hall, to get the whole picture and when she did, she cried out in shock.

"Oh, my God!"

Her husband Dan woke up long enough to shout, "What?" but when he saw through half-shut, myopic eyes that she was neither hanging from the ceiling fan nor lying naked and bloody from knife wounds, he promptly fell back to sleep.

This reassured Tookie until she remembered that her husband had stopped noticing anything about her a couple of years earlier.

Born Karen Basch thirty-six years ago, her mother called her Cookie, which her four-year-old sister Monica pronounced "Tookie," and Tookie stuck. Monica was tall like her mother and father, five foot eight by the time she reached fourteen, but Tookie was a runt, stopping her climb toward stature at a diminutive five foot three.

Tookie sat back down on her side of the bed and began to cry, her enlarged hands laying palms up in her lap like halibut fillets.

"Oh my, oh my," she said.

Dan mumbled something about coffee and then reached over to the night table, first for his glasses and then for the clock to see if he could steal a few more minutes of sleep. He didn't have to be at Deloitte and Touche, where he was a Senior Accountant, until 9:20.

"Dan? Danny? Could you turn over and take a look at me?"

Her husband rolled over without curiosity and faced his wife's hunched-over back.

"What?"

She stood up and turned around to face him, her pale green nightgown barely reaching her meatless thighs. Her arms had lengthened toward her knees, which now looked knobby, and her legs, once thick with muscle from thousands of miles on the treadmill, had stretched into slender ropes.

"Holy shit."

2.

They sat in Dr. Blechner's waiting room without an appointment because this was an emergency, Dan insisted, and they damn well needed some answers.

Dr. Blechner didn't have any.

"Good heavens," he said when he saw this woman he'd known for more than a decade. Tookie was wearing a pair of her husband's trousers that looked on her like capri pants and a red plaid flannel shirt with unbuttoned sleeves that barely surpassed her elbows. The doctor checked Tookie's heart and lungs, took a urine sample, and then drew blood, shaking his head several times in the process as if shaking would jostle the situation into perspective.

"Have you ever seen anything like this before, Doctor?" Dan asked.

"Well…" Dr. Blechner said, pulling on one of his earlobes, "I've seen pictures of acromegaly in the textbooks. But I don't think this is acromegaly."

"Am I going to die?" Tookie asked, trying not to cry. She felt sure her condition was fatal.

"No, no," Dr. Blechner said reassuringly, but in truth he didn't have the slightest idea.

3.

For the first time since their marriage six years earlier, Dan went clothes shopping with his wife.

"You can't go around wearing my clothes," he said. "They look ridiculous and they don't even fit."

"I'm sorry," Tookie said as if she'd backed the car into their garbage cans or shrunk his favorite sweater.

He should have said it wasn't her fault but he wasn't convinced that was true. *She must have done something wrong*, he thought, but he just couldn't imagine what.

4.

After Dan dropped Tookie off at home, hurrying downtown to his office in the Chicago Loop, she floated around their Sheridan Road condo like a stranger who'd wandered into someone else's life. Feeling a little dizzy, perhaps from the altitude, Tookie sat down in the breakfast nook with her coffee and peanut buttered bagel and stared at her iPhone in the charger. She felt that she should call somebody but she could not think of what to say. *Oh, hi, mom, guess what, I just grew two feet last night while I was sleeping.* She knew better than to give an hysteric like her mother a reason to become hysterical, and this was a really good reason. Of course, she would eventually have to tell her family. But now that Monica's 40th birthday had been put to rest, she didn't expect to see them for a while, which was fine with her.

Tookie decided to call her friend Wanda. Bizarre as it sounds, Wanda had been abducted by aliens from the Leda 25177 galaxy in the Hydra Supercluster when she was a pimply-faced teenager. They returned her to earth with clear skin and the formula for a spongy white mud that cured acne, which her parents subsequently sold to Merle Norman for a very large undisclosed amount. Tookie felt sure that Wanda, who, thanks to the abduction, was now independently wealthy, would know how to put Tookie's transformation in perspective.

"When I woke up this morning, I was seven feet tall," Tookie said when Wanda answered.

"Are you at work?"

"No. I called in sick." Tookie usually called Wanda from her office at Leo Burnett, where she was an advertising media buyer.

"Are you sick?"

"No, but I'm seven feet tall, Wanda. Actually six foot eleven and a fourth. The doctor measured me."

"You went to see the doctor?"

"Dan thought a doctor would know what was going on."

"Did he know?"

"No, he wasn't sure."

"It's God's mysterious will," Wanda said, which was what she always said when strange things happened.

"Dan had to buy me a bunch of new clothes. He went with me to Marshall Field's."

"Well, that's good," Wanda said. "They have a lot of nice things at Field's."

5.

For the rest of the day, Tookie explored the upper half of the condominium. She replaced the burned out bulbs in the dining room chandelier, the track lights in the living room, and the carriage lamp in the entryway. She dusted the tops of the bookcases, which had not been touched since she and Dan moved in. She pruned and watered the hanging plants on the balcony, and she tackled the floor-to-ceiling windows with vinegar and newspaper.

Then she went outside and took a walk. She touched the soft, moist leaf buds that were opening on the oak tree branches, peeked into a robin's nest and counted three spotted blue eggs, and observed that most of the neighboring rain gutters were clogged with winter debris. She also discovered that she scared small dogs and startled old women, most of whom could only make eye contact with her navel. And every so often, if she stood on her toes, she caught a glimpse of the silver gray waters of Lake Michigan. Tookie began to think that short people were as tragically handicapped as the deaf and blind, and imagined organizing a fund raiser to promote compassion and understanding for the vertically challenged. Waking up tall, she thought, was certainly not the worst thing that could happen to a person.

6.

That night, Tookie put on the new black extra-long Marshall Fields nightie that Dan had bought her and for the first time in six years tried to initiate their lovemaking.

"I'm a different woman now, Danny. Don't you think we should re-consummate our marriage?"

"I don't know," Dan said, shying away from her. At five foot nine, he barely came to the top of her chest. "You feel like a stranger to me, Took, I can't help it."

"I thought men liked new women," she said.

"Not this new," Dan said.

"Well, it's not new down there," she said.

"How do you know?" he said. "Everything else is different."

"Not my breasts," she said.

"That's true," Dan agreed sadly.

"You're such a shit," Tookie said, surprising herself with the exclamation, and she wanted to say even more. But instead she just crawled into the bed, which was now a foot too short for her legs, and wept.

7.

Tookie woke up very early the next morning and got into the office at 7:30. After Dan's reaction the night before, she was determined to avoid attention. But when The Morning Show caterer went past her office in the hallway at 9:30, Tookie called to her, hoping that if she stayed seated, the girl wouldn't notice her height. Tookie craved something sweet like a cinnamon bun or a maple bar and now that she was as tall as a Chicago Bulls shooting guard, she could eat anything she wanted without worrying about getting fat. It would have been great if only her height weren't quite so extreme. Six feet would have been plenty, she thought, but her predicament was like Alice and the eat-me pills.

Almost the same thing had happened to Tookie when she was twelve and wished for breasts. She went from nothing to a C-cup practically overnight, and got teased for being "chesty." Then she lost *too* much of it when she was on Weight Watchers in her twenties, and never got it back. You had to be careful what you wished for, she thought, making a mental note.

Fortunately, the lunch date she'd scheduled was with a new client, NaturalCat Organic Cat Food, so he wouldn't look shocked when she met him at the restaurant. She spent all morning tweaking her media plan, carefully addressing the changes her boss Luther had requested to beef up the organic-only pubs. She stopped only long enough to learn that all her medical tests had come back normal and to respond to Wanda's text message urging her to contact Oprah or Dr. Oz.

At noon, Tookie left the agency by a side door, feeling relieved that she'd survived the morning without being outed.

8.

Evan Collier was waiting for her at the bar when she arrived at The Gage, one of the trendy new downtown lunch venues. She was relieved to see that his cocktail was a Perrier with lime, because her last Cat client had been a raging alcoholic. Better still, Collier was tall, over six feet two, she estimated, although he only came up to her chin.

"Delighted to meet you," he said, grasping her hand and looking her over like she was a brand new Maserati. He had the kind of man's face that usually came with a dusty Stetson and a big open sky. Tookie had been stooping a little when she approached him, but his smile made her stand up straight.

9.

How she ended up at the Hotel Sofitel Water Tower that afternoon, wrapped in Evan Collier's burly arms, she could not explain—although the two apple martinis she downed probably smoothed the way. She had not only betrayed her husband, she had violated a cardinal rule of business. Of course, she knew that plenty of people, including her boss Luther, violated that rule, but it was so unlike Tookie. What was it about being tall that had changed her so profoundly? And the worst of it was that she wasn't even sorry. She hadn't let herself realize until today how neglected she'd felt, how unnoticed and unappreciated by Dan. This man, Evan Collier, had made love to her like she was a gorgeous, sensual gazelle, delighting in her long limbs and soft skin and sweet taste. No, she definitely was not sorry. And if he asked her to join him for another romantic rendezvous, or even a runaway weekend in Belize, she just might say yes, and yes, and yes.

10.

When Tookie returned to Leo Burnett late that afternoon, she no longer tried to hide. She strode through the lobby with a big smile on her face and laughed with enjoyment when the receptionist gaped at her. *Get used to it*, she thought.

"What the hell *happened* to you?" her boss Luther said when she came into his office. "You look like a goddam flamingo!"

"I had a growth spurt," she said, and sat down in his love seat, crossing her legs in the becoming manner that only tall, skinny women execute properly. "By the way, the lunch went well. Evan signed off on the media plan without any changes."

"Really? I heard he was a sonovabitch," Luther said, holding his stubbly jowls in the cup of his hand.

"Not to me," Tookie said, smiling provocatively. She knew Luther wouldn't believe what she'd been up to that afternoon even if she showed him a videotape, but it was fun to tease him a little.

"What the hell happened to *you*?" he said again with a low, soft whistle.

11.

That night, after Tookie slid under the covers with her husband, she said, "we'll have to get a bigger bed, honey."

"Maybe you'll wake up tomorrow and be short again," Dan said, continuing to read the latest Alex Cross mystery. He seemed to have lost interest in his wife's predicament once Dr. Blechner couldn't diagnose it.

"I wouldn't count on it," Tookie said, although the thought made her a little anxious.

"Well, we'll just have to make the best of it," he said, which was Dan's way of telling her he had stopped listening.

12.

Later that night, Tookie's cold toes woke her up and she went into the kitchen to make herself a cup of herbal tea. She augmented it with a slice of red velvet birthday cake left over from her sister Monica's party, scraping the remnants of cream cheese frosting off the plate with her fork.

In the soft light of the kitchen dimmers, she examined her legs and arms, stretching them out to their full lengths and taking deep, relaxing breaths. *Goddam flamingo!* she thought, smiling at the recollection. She realized that this bizarre transformation had given her more than height. It had given her perspective, enabled her to— what was that expression?—to see the forest for the trees. And she knew that even if she woke up five foot three again tomorrow morning, she would not be the same woman she used to be. She intended to ask more of Dan, to insist that he rise to her occasion. She would no longer mouse around like a timid housemaid, or let him treat her like a footstool he only noticed when he tripped over it.

The stove clock said 2:10, but she did not feel pressured to return to bed. She savored all the tiny sounds that punctuated the night's silence, the refrigerator motor, the ice maker, a window's hoarse rattle as a car sped past outside, even the soft click of the clock hand to 2:11.

Tookie decided that her friend Wanda was right. Whatever happened, it was God's mysterious will. *Somebody's* mysterious will at any rate, she thought, embracing the mystery without fear. And while it meant that some poor soul in Prague might wake up one morning as a cockroach, on a different morning a hundred years later, a short woman in Chicago could just as well wake up tall.

L E S L E Y   K I M B A L L

The Beginning of the End

When the bees first arrived, there was no precedent.
Vinyl-bottomed, hovering machines with no interest
in me or the gardens I was trying to recreate.
Seismic buzzing following me into my new house,
my new bed, sending me downtown to seek refuge.
The next spring when nothing was new, I noticed holes
in the wood, seeping brown juice and too small
for the armored bees, yet they disappeared this way.
Carpenters, my sister declared, and *nothing to be done.*
I ignored them, stayed out of the yard in the afternoons,
it felt natural to pretend nothing was wrong.
Cicadas kept me company in late summer, singing
harvest songs while I carried sun-warm tomatoes
into the kitchen, filled the freezer with red sauce,
enough for several winters, more than I would ever eat.
Who could tell how deep the bees had tunneled?
Shouldn't carpenters be building, I thought after spilling red wine
on the borrowed couch, counting the days until I could begin.

MELISSA FERGUSON

Michelangelo's Veins

This seems like a good time to wash my underwear. I've finished my
burger and salad and I'm not rostered on for clean-up duty. Most of
the girls had their showers before dinner, so the toilet block should
be quiet. No one to talk to, or smile at, or get to know, no fun to be
had or moments to be seized; just me and my undies. I get up from
the table and scrape shreds of lettuce into the scrap bin and dump my
plate and cutlery into a tub. As I walk past the oafs in the picnic area
I look down and pretend to inspect my fingernails.

The warm, moist air in the cinder-block bathroom reminds me of
disembarking a plane in the tropics. I imagine droplets of moisture,
loaded with sweat and flakes of skin, settling all over me and
entering my lungs. This is how diseases spread.

One of the toilet doors is closed. I listen for a tell-tale rustle,
tinkle, cough or fart. All I hear is the buzz of mosquitos and the thud
of moths slamming into the flickering fluorescent light.

We left the last concrete-and-dirt European camping ground
early this morning and arrived at this concrete-and-dirt camping
ground late this afternoon. Our bus is connecting the dots on a
cartoon map of Europe; I don't expect any meaningful picture to
emerge. As soon as the bus departed this morning all the hung-over
passengers fell asleep with gasping fish mouths. After a nap the party
resumed; people sauntered from seat to seat or twisted around to
chat. I put on my headphones and soothed myself listening to a
hardcore punk playlist. I closed my eyes and visualised the bus
driver slamming on the brakes and pitching one of the dickheads

standing in the aisle through the windscreen. On arrival at the camping ground I took a cabin with Jenna. She's probably tired of being stuck with killjoy me. She's like some blonde, tanned, mineral make-up commercial, while I'm more of a Government Health Warning label.

On the first day of the tour Jenna thought sitting up the back of the bus would be cool, as if we're still in high school. We compromised and have claimed seats just back from the middle. Most nights I go to bed before her. She stays up and drinks with all the others. A hangover reminds me too much of chemotherapy.

I rinse out the concrete sink, remove hair from the plug using a square of toilet paper, dump in my underwear and plug the sink hole with a sock. Someone sobs behind the closed toilet door. Can't I even have five minutes to myself? I turn on the tap to drown out the noise, and mix a soup of bras, knickers, and socks.

Jenna came to me bearing the brochure as I neared the end of treatment. Vibrant pictures of young people, balancing the Eiffel Tower in the palm of their hand or pushing over the Leaning Tower of Pisa with a single finger filled the glossy pages. The brochure promised that 98.1% of past travellers surveyed 'had fun'. I wanted fun. At the time I thought the end of treatment would be something to celebrate. I thought I'd be one of those *Ambassadors for Life* whose brave brush with death enables them to cherish every moment. Instead now I'm broken. Most people my age are oblivious and smug and still believe they can be anything they want to be. For me life has been soiled like a white debutante dress smeared with dust and beer and cigarette ash.

Behind me, in the toothpaste-spotted mirror, I see the stall door open. I look down into the sink and put on my best fuck-off expression. A figure shuffles forward and stops about a metre behind me. I scrub at the gusset of a pair of knickers with a block of soap. The person sniffs and takes another step forward. Nicole catches my eyes in the mirror. Nicole is one half of a kiwi couple. She and her husband Aaron must be pushing the upper age limit for this 18-35-

year-olds' tour. Her face is swollen and blurry like a newspaper left in the rain. I sigh and turn to face her.

'Sorry. I'm just so upset. I don't know what to do,' Nicole says in a voice that sounds as though she's just sucked on helium.

'Why? What's happened?'

'I'm not pregnant... again.' She pushes something toward me.

It's one of those pregnancy test sticks. I don't want to look at it or touch it. It seems kind of personal and it has been dipped in her urine. Instead I look at her face and say, 'Have you and Aaron been trying to have a baby?'

Her face becomes a marionette controlled by invisible strings. Tears ooze out of the corners of her eyes. This is exactly the sort of thing I want to avoid, the reason I don't want to get involved with these people. I have enough of my own misery without taking on theirs as well. Nicole brings her hands up to her face and takes another step toward me. Is this the part where I'm supposed to comfort her? I pat her shoulder. I'm not going to give her a hug. She wipes a sleeve across her eyes and sniffs up some snot.

'Yes, for almost a year now. Everyone says conception can take up to a year.'

'Really?' I say. I can't see the big deal about children. The ones I know are all illogical, repetitive, boring, and moody; equivalent to small drunks.

'Yeah. Now I should probably see a doctor to find out what's wrong with me.'

'Probably. There might be something they can do.'

'Everywhere I look people are holding babies and women's bellies are popping out. It's just not fair. It seems so easy for everybody else. I thought if we came on this trip I wouldn't think about it and it might just happen. But I can't stop thinking about it.'

Nicole seems the mum type. She always knows the right thing to say and the appropriate way to act. I've seen her hold back the hair of a vomiting girl and she always tells the young guys when they've had too much to drink. Before everything happened to me, I did expect that one day, I would become the kind of woman who wanted children.

'There's a chance I may never be able to have children.'

I can't believe I just told her that. I don't want anyone's sympathy. Nicole does know about my illness. Jenna informed some people early on in the tour, probably in defence of my anti-social behaviour. In a way I was glad because it explained my neo-Nazi hairstyle.

'I had a friend who had umm... leukaemia I think. She went on to have children,' Nicole says.

'Yeah. I've heard of lots of people too. Every type of treatment's different. The doctors were definite. They asked me if I wanted to freeze some eggs.'

'Did you?'

'Nah. Just sounded like more time in hospital to me.'

I remember the purgatory of hospital waiting rooms. Not being able to talk or eat or read. Just focussed on hearing my name called and hardening myself to endure the ordeal to come.

Nicole and I watch a cockroach crawl toward the drain in the middle of the floor.

'Sometimes I think maybe there's some big secret... to getting pregnant. I mean like sex isn't really how you do it. Like there's another hole somewhere and all this penis and vagina thing's a myth.'

Nicole smiles, so I laugh. Then she laughs too.

'Anyway, sorry to burden you. Thanks for listening. And don't give up hope. When you're ready I'm sure you'll find a way to have children.' She holds her arms out toward me.

I lean my body forward so she can give me a hug. I'm careful to avoid the pissy pregnancy stick in her hand.

'Come to my cabin when you're done here. A couple of us girls are having a quiet night. We're going to play cards. Jenna's coming.'

'Okay. Yeah, maybe. Thanks. I'll just finish washing these.'

Nicole blows her nose on a piece of toilet paper and splashes water on her face, then leaves the bathroom. I turn back to the sink, pick up a sock and the soap and scrub.

I think I'll give cards a miss. I really can't get involved in any more life dramas. I can't be anyone's shoulder to cry on. My shoulder turned from warm flesh to stone when white-coats filled my veins with litres of cold chemicals. I'll just go back to the cabin, read a book and eat a block of the chocolate I bought in Switzerland. At least if Jenna's out I won't have to share.

I give my socks and underpants Chinese-burns to squeeze the water from them and hang them on the communal washing line. On my way back I stop in front of Nicole's cabin. All the cabins are in a row, identical faces with no personality like robots pretending to be human. The window is a closed eye and the door a mouth through which I can hear Jenna's hiccoughing laugh. I used to make her laugh. I'd rub melted chocolate on my front teeth, then smile at her showing my 'peasant teeth'. She'd crack up every time.

Jenna and I had planned trips like this since we were thirteen. We thought we'd see the world before we came home to get married, have babies and wear high-heels to our high-powered executive jobs. Now we're here on the other side of the world. I guess I'm lucky I actually made it. One day when I went in for chemotherapy a woman I'd seen before but never spoken to sat across from me in the waiting room. On this day she had a little girl, with black curly hair, on the chair next to her. Probably her daughter. In front of her a baby doll sat in a pink stroller. The woman smiled and laughed as though they were at the zoo or out for a milkshake. 'Now Dolly has to stay there and not move,' the woman said and her daughter giggled and repeated the words. I couldn't imagine bringing a child to the hospital, their face and name and the sound of their voice would be forever linked with chemotherapy.

Then the woman looked up at me and said, 'Nice hat.'

I had on a khaki cap with a red star embroidered on the front. I called it my socialist revolutionary cap.

'Thanks. I see your hair's growing back.'

She had a short crop of black hair so I assumed she'd finished her treatment and was recovering.

'Not for long. I'm starting treatment again today. The thought of it makes me sick to my stomach.' Her mouth turned down at the edges.

'Oh.'

'I'm on the research stuff now.'

'Oh.'

'There's not much they can do for me.'

Her daughter kicked her chubby legs in the air. I couldn't speak. There were no appropriate or comforting words or platitudes I could muster. I looked around the room. Anywhere but at her face. I fiddled with the buckle on my bag and cleared my throat. I'd be okay. I'd travel around Europe, like I'd always planned, while this woman, with a small child to look after, would die. How does that work?

Insects scurry into the corners when I switch on the light in my cabin. I flop down on the bottom bunk and reach into the front pocket of my backpack to pull out my chocolate. My book's on the pillow. I open it, the bookmark falls onto my chest. It's a postcard of Michelangelo's David. We saw him in Florence a couple of camping-grounds ago. I hold the postcard up above my head then close my eyes and retrace my steps through the gallery towards David. By the time I reached him he towered above me. Michelangelo had carved muscle and bone and skin into the marble. I traced the ropey veins with my eyes and stroked the crook of my elbow—where my own veins had disintegrated. I thought David would just be another tourist attraction rip-off, a big statue of a naked bloke. Michelangelo liberated the life hidden within a chunk of cold, lifeless stone. I place David back inside my book and close it. Holding the chocolate in front of me, I walk out the cabin door and back towards the laughter calling from Nicole's cabin.

ROLAND PEASE

Pretty Please, or Life is Short

Stop with the inanities. Our very world is coming to an end and you are mouthing off, telling me why it's better to shop here instead of there. You are driving me crazy, and there's only moments left. Let me be. Let me be lost in thought. Let me linger on ideas of merit. I would leave you in the lurch, but we are trapped in this elevator together, and the cables are snapping. I hear them twanging and it's no joke. I'd choke you, but I'm not that sort. Put a lid on it right this minute. Damn. There goes another one, sweet Jesus of mine.

Portrait #1

That dunderhead was so blasé.
He schlepped his way across
the room in his zombie trance
and demanded us to take him
seriously. Expecting someone
with grace and manners, we
were dismayed. His shirtfront
was disheveled, his hair askew,
and his expression hard to read.
He looked as if he had had too
much to drink, yet he was holding a can of Pepsi. He's someone
I must answer to in the long run
if I want to maintain my career.
He's in charge of operations, such
as they are. He did make a snide
remark that I found funny, and I
could see he enjoyed my enjoyment.
I wonder how he was able to climb up
the ladder to his current status. He does
not look like he has much on the ball at all.
His name is Roger and he has a weary looking
wife named Abigail who enjoys her Dubonnet. I
saw her going after the drink with great enthusiasm.
Roger said he liked curling, polo and strip joints, which
certainly put a stop to the conversation. I have a feeling
I'll be looking for a new job before long, but there is always
a chump wherever you go. Just seems to be the case. I am not
good at holding things in, and someday I'll tell him what a jerk
he is, how he's driving his wife to drink, is sloppy with his shirt.

JOHN BIGGS

End Times Confusion

Mona's mother said the world would come to an end pretty soon. Maybe not today or tomorrow, but in a year or two. That's why girls from good Choctaw families were turning into lesbians.

"End times confusion," she told Mona. "I heard it on the radio." There weren't many Choctaw lesbians yet, but by the time Gabriel dusted off his horn there'd be truckloads of Indian girls doing lesbian things with other Indian girls.

"I just hope Jesus understands."

When Mona asked which exact passage in the Bible condemned girls loving girls, Mom told her, "The Hebrew language had no nasty words, so all the lesbian verses were written between the lines."

Mom explained how all the important biblical women were either whores or wives when they quit being virgins. And if that wasn't proof enough, there was that part about being fruitful and replenishing the earth.

"Hate the sin but love the sinner," Mom said. "Especially when she's your daughter." Mona's parents wouldn't throw her out, or refuse to speak to her, but they felt duty bound to disapprove.

The worst thing was the sad way Mom and Dad looked at her. The way Mom introduced her to suitable men. The way Dad pretended she'd forget all this sexual foolishness in a few years.

He said she had the right kind of hips for making babies. He blushed when he said it. Choctaw fathers don't talk about their daughters that way, even when the girls were natural beauties like Mona. Her long black hair looked like it had been coated with gelatin, her deep brown eyes could swallow a man's self control, and the way she walked made young men turn their heads.

Dad said, "I see them watching you."

Mona couldn't tell if that made him proud or angry. A little of both, she decided. Her dad was a man, after all. A better man than most; he'd provide for her, and protect her. He'd step in front of a bullet or a charging bull, or a runaway train if it came to that, but he couldn't wrap his mind around the idea of lesbian love.

"You're a pretty girl." Dad held up one finger like he was counting up her assets. Like he was describing a prize mule he had for sale, but Mona was more complicated than livestock.

"A really pretty girl." He held up a second finger to keep the first one company.

"A really, really pretty girl." He held up a third finger. Three good reasons for Mona to get married and start having babies instead of letting her ovaries fall to earth like overripe apples.

"You've got it all," her father said. "You're beautiful, desirable, practically Miss America. Why can't you love a man?"

"Why can't you?" Mona knew Dad would never get it. She'd seen herself in the mirror; she knew how attractive she was to men, but those features made some women want her too. Her legs, her breasts, her narrow waist, her bubble butt, and especially her face. According to her best friend Chris, Mona's looks made her a lipstick lesbian who didn't need lipstick.

Dad knew what she was thinking; Dad always knew what she was thinking.

"Chris is almost a man," he said. "But she ain't made it all the way."

Choctaw knew about women with warrior spirits. A cosmic mistake made by Chitokaka, *The Great One*, before the Europeans came and convinced him to be a Baptist. Mona wasn't one of those warrior women. She didn't like hunting or fishing. Her muscles weren't strong. She couldn't fight. And most especially, Mona wanted to have babies; she just didn't want a man to be part of the process.

It was all very confusing, and depressing, especially a few days before her period, when her body reminded her she was a woman by making her cry for the slightest reason. Maybe girls like Mona *were* a sign of the last days, like Mom said. Maybe the end of the world would be Mona's fault, somehow, and "God made me this way" wouldn't be an acceptable excuse.

Chris told her to toughen up, or lighten up, or cheer up, depending on the route Mona's depression took and how Chris was feeling at the moment. Chris couldn't understand because she was one of those women with a warrior's spirit. She'd never understand the baby-wanting part. All Mona could do was think about her mixed up life, and cry. Women are never free of men, even women like Mona who don't want men for lovers, or women like Chris who walk and talk like men and take a man's first name, and get their hair cut in men's barber shops.

Men are rough. Men are crude. Men want to do disgusting things that give a woman not one ounce of pleasure. They'll slap girls on the bottom and pinch them in soft places, and tell them, "You like it, don't you sugar britches."

"The only reason women put up with men is having babies," Mona told Chris.

"We can't do it without them. Sex with a man is the price we have to pay."

"Toughen up." Chris snapped just like a man.

"That's the way things are." But Chris had a solution. Girls like Chris—and men—always have solutions.

"Turkey baster babies," she explained. All they needed was a few tablespoons of sperm and a way to squirt it inside of Mona at exactly the right time.

"You are even more disgusting than a man," Mona told her.

"Just trying to help," Chris said.

Men were always eager to help when it came to nasty things, but Chris's suggestion gave Mona an idea. There was a fertility clinic in Tulsa, and a girl could go there and get a tablespoon full of sperm put inside her at exactly the right time by a doctor with a special instrument that looked nothing like a penis. A female doctor, who might not be a lesbian, but at least she was a woman. At least she wouldn't tell Mona that the end of the world was coming and that's why girls liked girls. All Mona needed was a negative HIV test and $350.

"Comes complete with an ovulation test kit and an anonymous sperm donor with a college education," She told Chris.

"What kind of man donates his sperm?" Chris asked.

"Men leave their sperm all over the world," Mona said. "In the back seats of cars, in public restrooms and hotel rooms, inside of vaginas that never wanted it. Why wouldn't a perfectly ordinary man donate his sperm to a good cause?"

"Like blood," Chris said.

"Or corneas," Mona said.

"I still don't like it." Chris thought a turkey baster and a couple of gay male friends of hers might be better.

"They have lots of sperm," she said, and they'd do it free anytime we wanted.

Artificial insemination cost three hundred and fifty dollars for each attempt, but the doctors were careful, and generous with their anonymous college-educated sperm, and Mona got pregnant on the very first try.

When she finally got around to telling Mom and Dad, she pretended the baby had been started in the normal way.

"Let them think I'm a fallen woman," she told Chris. Mom and Dad would be happy to believe she'd slipped and landed on her back in the appropriate position to make a baby. That kind of thing happened all the time and they'd feel better about premarital sex than they would about artificial insemination. Much better.

Chris kept on about gay friends and turkey basters and how she felt left out of the whole process, especially since Mona didn't even let her come to the fertility clinic, "when the deed was done."

"The deed." Mona didn't like the way Chris looked at her belly, like there was some alien creature inside of her that had nothing to do with Chris, or love, or even the end of the world. Maybe it had something to do with the fact that Mona hadn't told her she was pregnant until people started wondering how she got so plump, and if she'd found a breast enlargement lotion that really worked.

She didn't let Chris come for the sonogram either.

"The doctors couldn't see a penis." They told her she should try again just to be sure, but it looked like she was carrying a little girl.

"Exactly what I wanted," Mona said. "Why push my luck when things are going well?"

"This baby will have two mothers," she told Chris. "A little girl with two mommies." Mona could already picture her daughter in dresses and ribbons, a miniature lipstick lesbian just like momma Mona.

If Chris had baby fantasies, she didn't say, but Mona was determined her daughter wouldn't be anything like Chris. No butch haircut or men's clothes, or fistfights. She'd be strong and self sufficient, but in a feminine way, and she'd be pretty like Mona, and smart like her college educated anonymous father. She'd have enough Choctaw blood to qualify for the roles, but enough white blood that banks would give her credit.

"Left out," Chris said. "That's how I feel."

And that feeling got worse as the weeks rolled by and Mona looked less like Miss America and more like a pumpkin with legs. She got florid stretch marks in spite of the cocoa butter. Her face filled up with hormone-enriched fluids. Her emotions teetered on bipolar disorder, and she urinated sixteen times a day.

"Stretch marks fade," she told Chris. "Fluid retention goes away. Hormone levels recede to pre-flood levels. Everything will get back to normal except we'll have a darling little girl."

"Darling." Chris didn't say that word very often.

"Getting back to normal." She didn't say that often either, because there was nothing normal about Chris and Mona—not in Choctaw country anyway—and having a darling little girl around would make things even less normal than before.

"I don't think things are working out," Chris said, talking like a man again.

"I think we should start seeing other people. You need some Mona time. It's not you, it's me." Only a butch-lesbian like Chris could get away with so many cross-gender clichés.

"You're leaving me," Mona said, already crying, already feeling the baby's feet against her ribs, already needing to visit the bathroom for the third time in an hour.

Chris's sense of timing was perfectly masculine. She looked at her watch with its studded leather band and said, "I've got to go right now."

She headed for the front door of the little frame house that Mona couldn't afford to rent without her. She stopped long enough to say, "I'll be back for my things later. See ya."

Wouldn't want to be ya. Mona knew Mom and Dad would help her if they could, but they couldn't help her very long. And she'd have to listen to them tell her everything happened for the best, except for her passing lesbian phase. They'd talk to her about paternity tests, because they didn't know about the anonymous college educated sperm donor. They'd talk to her about Aid to Dependent Children, and tribal money, and Mom would talk about the end of the world, which was still on the way but might have been pushed back another year or two thanks to Mona's miraculous pregnancy.

It really was miraculous, because Mona was pregnant, but still a virgin. Maybe this baby would be the second coming of Jesus, like the Bible predicted, only this time the Messiah would be a lipstick lesbian.

End times really were confusing.

WENDELL SMITH

Just As My Fetus Felt

Just as my fetus felt
"There isn't womb enough for me!"
before it jumped from out the Golden Gate
between my mother's thighs
and I began my free fall
through this materiality,
so now I feel constrained by lack of time.

Time, which passed too slowly
to be noticed in my youth,
has been accelerated into visibility
by the gravity of death.
And, although time's limit has always been,
it seems so much, so more so, now;
it compels me to streamline my soul,
and prepare it for its plunge
through the surface tension
of the event horizon,
at the fluid boundary,
between this airy time of mine,
and the black lit whole
of liquid timelessness
which is to be
our new singularity.

Fractal Caveat

The best of poems
are sung and lost
they form and vanish
like the fingers of frost
that come to craze
the edges of a pond
on early mornings
of late autumn days.

Advance Directive

I have seen enough of death at work,
enough of nursing homes
and other prisons,
of wards, intensive, careful and careless—
to wish to leave my body well behind
before I come to leave my mind.

So, my friends, I make us this suggestion:
let's choose, as I am choosing now;
may we embrace pneumonia
or whatever *It* may choose to use
to throw us out upon the universe
to wend our way until we reach
the gods of Betelgeuse and those beyond.
For what reason should we cling
to our bodies beyond the season
of our grandchildren's spring?

Do we not love them
and, therefore, owe to them
the air we breathe
the earth we walk upon
the water that we drink?
Think! Think!
What a burden we would be to them
if we should live forever;
loving, we must leave them
room for their life's endeavor.

WILLIAM OGDEN HAYNES

Window Dressing

His neighbors would always say
he was lucky to have the only house
on the street that was covered in ivy.
They said that ivy was idyllic
as it grew on the hallowed halls
of academia and fairy tale
cottages in sylvan glades.
His house made the street look
pastoral, Arcadian and picturesque.

But what the hell did the neighbors know?
They didn't have to live
in the ivy-smothered cottage
where he couldn't even see
through the bedroom window
nearly blocked by a frame of foliage.
He could almost sense the ivy
moving against the outer walls
and trying to get inside by growing
around the window screens.
And one pivotal day, he noticed the tendrils
metastasize around the pillars on the front porch
and encroach onto the concrete patio.

So, he took a cooler of beer outside,
put on some garden gloves
and began to pull on the vines
under the watchful gaze of his neighbors.
When the ivy was pulled away,

it left thousands of little feet
still anchored to the house like leeches,
and beneath, he could see the destruction of shutters,
window sashes, screens and siding.
After the vines were piled in the street,
the people watched as he pressure-washed
the house and sprayed copious amounts
of herbicide near the foundation.
And during the next two days of painting,
no one talked to him or gave a friendly wave.
But neither did they take advantage
of the offer on his yard sign that said,
Free ivy available for transplantation.

JOANNA M. WESTON

Rebuilding

the sound of wrecking bar
and saw
punctuate the lines
of my poem

the rhythm of work
pulses through my thoughts
to become the day's syncopation

I listen   watch
the sway of trees
and consider how wood
frames this house
and room after room emerges
under your hammer

RUTH MARGOLIN SILIN

The String Puller

On a beach in Miami folks
applaud the setting sun like
a curtain falling on the second
act of a Broadway play—while
up North on a Cambridge street
children watch costumed marionettes
make silly moves—and they never see
behind the curtain, a String Puller
making magic.

CONTRIBUTOR NOTES

NINA RUBINSTEIN ALONSO's poetry has appeared in *Ploughshares*, *The New Yorker*, *The New Boston Review*, etc. and her book, *This Body*, was published by Godine Press. Her story "Fire Pit" appears in the *Southern Women's Review*. She directs Fresh Pond Ballet, has taught at Boston Ballet, and also loves meditation and growing basil and stringless French beans in her garden. Her dear daughter Lara is at UVM. She seeks the transformative energy of art, squeezing thoughts and words until the juice rises. She can be reached at ninaralonso@gmail.com.

SYLVIA ASHBY's background is in theatre—both acting and writing. She has published 15 scripts for family audiences. Her recent memoir on Anderbo.com put her in the mood to do something with her poems. Her only Boston connection: she spent summers with her aunt in Chelsea, mostly studying the odd-shaped pasta in Italian groceries, buying a 15 cent ricotta-filled pastry from the Italian bakeries, or eating pizza long before it became one of the four basic food groups.

PEGGY AYLSWORTH is a retired psychotherapist, 92, living in Santa Monica, CA with her poet/blogger husband, Norm Levine. Her poetry has appeared in numerous literary journals throughout the U.S. and abroad, including *Poetry Salzburg Review*, *Beloit Poetry Journal*, and *The MacGuffin*. Her work was nominated for the 2012 Pushcart Prize.

JOHN BIGGS is a broad spectrum fiction writer with about 25 stories published in journals that vary from *Kansas City Voices* and *Midwestern Gothic* to *Disturbed Digest*. He was the grand prize winner of the 80th annual *Writer's Digest* competition and the third prize winner of the 2011 Lorian Hemingway short story contest. His first novel, *Owl Dreams*, will be released by Pen-L Publishing later this year.

ACE BOGGESS is author of two collections of poetry: *The Prisoners* (forthcoming from Brick Road Poetry Press) and *The Beautiful Girl Whose Wish Was Not Fulfilled* (Highwire Press, 2003). His writing has appeared in *Harvard Review, Mid-American Review, Atlanta Review, RATTLE, River Styx, Southern Humanities Review*, and many other journals. He currently resides in Charleston, West Virginia.

CATHY BRYANT's poems and stories have been published all over the world since her best friend blackmailed her into submitting them. She only sent them to magazines to prove to him that no one would want them. She was delighted to be wrong. In 2012 Cathy won the Bulwer-Lytton Fiction Contest and three poetry contests. In 2013 she won the M.R. Jordan Short Fiction prize. Cathy co-edits the anthology *Best of Manchester Poets*, and her own collection, *Contains Strong Language and Scenes of a Sexual Nature*, was published recently. Cathy also does a monthly listing of free writing competitions and calls for submission for the "Write Out Loud Community" group. Contact her at cathy@cathybryant.co.uk—and yes, she bought her best friend a drink or two.

VALENTINA CANO is a student of classical singing who spends whatever free time either writing or reading. Her works have appeared in *Exercise Bowler, Blinking Cursor, Theory Train, Cartier Street Press, Berg Gasse 19, Precious Metals, A Handful of Dust, The Scarlet Sound, The Adroit Journal, Perceptions Literary Magazine, Welcome to Wherever, The Corner Club Press, Death Rattle, Danse Macabre, Subliminal Interiors, Generations Literary Journal, A Narrow Fellow, Super Poetry Highway, Stream Press, Stone Telling, Popshot, Ontologica, Pipe Dream, Decades Review, Anatomy, Lowestof Chronicle, Muddy River Poetry Review, Lady Ink Magazine, Spark Anthology, Awaken Consciousness Magazine, Vine Leaves Literary Magazine, Avalon Literary Review, Caduceus, White Masquerade Anthology*, and others. Her poetry has been nominated for Best of the Web and the Pushcart Prize. You can find her here: http://carabosseslibrary.blogspot.com.

MICHAEL COLLINS is a graduate of Kalamazoo College, the Warren Wilson College MFA Program for Writers, and Drew University. He teaches creative and expository writing at New York University. His work has recently appeared or will appear in *BlazeVOX, Dressing Room Poetry Journal, Red Savina Review, Blood Lotus Journal, Mobius: The Journal of Social Change, Grist: The Journal for Writers, Kenning Journal, Pank,* and *SOFTBLOW*. He lives in Mamaroneck, New York, with his wife, Carol.

KRIKOR DER HOHANNESIAN's poems have appeared in many literary journals, including *The Atlanta Review, Louisiana Literature,* and *Connecticut Review*. His first chapbook, *Ghosts and Whispers,* was published by Finishing Line Press in 2010 and nominated for The Pen New England Awards and Mass Book Awards, the latter selecting it as a "must read." A second chapbook, *Refuge in the Shadows,* was released in 2013 by Cervena Barva Press.

BILL DILL was more a reader than writer of poems over years teaching and practicing management in many settings around the world. Prose is no longer his necessary metier. With many others who come from life rather than MFA programs, he is enjoying the challenge of writing poems that others want to read and welcoming the lumps and cheers from critiques along the way by which one learns. He'll draw from mishaps in how men organize, from 60 years with best wife/best critic, from wisdom of his grandchildren, love of sea and mountains, and hope sometime for a glimpse of truth.

CARA EHLENFELDT is from Tabernacle, New Jersey. She would like to have conversations with Vergil, Catullus, and other Latin poets, but will settle for just reading their poems. Her poetry also appears in *Third Wednesday* and *The Waterhouse Review*.

KAREN ENGLISH has been a children's author for the past sixteen years. Her latest book is due out in December (Dog Days: The Carver Chronicles, Book One) with Clarion, an imprint of Houghton Mifflin. Her middle grade novel, Francie (Farrar, Straus, & Giroux -1999) won the Coretta Scott King Honor Award. However, her passion is short fiction.

MELISSA FERGUSON earns a living as a cancer-fighting scientist. She writes when her two children are finally in bed. Her writing has appeared in *Island*, *Mused*, and the *Sounds of Silence* anthology.

VIRGINIA BACH FOLGER lives in Schenectady, New York. Ginny has worked as a gas station attendant, paralegal, switchboard operator, claims adjuster, and corporate learning and development manager. When not writing poetry, she dabbles in her garden, collects old postcards, and dotes on her eight-year-old grandson. She has previously published in *Horticulture* magazine and *Misjudge Your Limits*, as well as in *Constellations: A Journal of Poetry and Fiction*.

E. A. FOW is originally from New Zealand but has been living and writing in New York City for over twenty years. Her work appears in anthologies from Softskull Press, Imagination & Place Press, and the forthcoming *Flash in the Attic* from Fiction Attic Press, as well as in various online journals such as *Penduline* and *RiverLit*. Links to stories and her bibliography can be found at EAFow.com.

BRANDON FRENCH has been assistant editor of *Modern Teen Magazine*, a topless Pink Pussycat cocktail waitress (that's another story!), assistant professor of English at Yale, a published film scholar, a playwright and screenwriter, director of development at Columbia Pictures Television, an award-winning advertising copywriter and creative director, a psychoanalyst in private practice, and a mother. Thirteen of her stories have been accepted for publication by literary journals and she was nominated for the Kirkwood Prize in Fiction at UCLA.

HARRIS GARDNER is the founder of the Boston National Poetry Month Festival and of the acclaimed literary organization Tapestry of Voices. His books include *Lest They Become* (Ibbetson Street Press) and *Among Us* (Cervena Barva Press), and his work has appeared in dozens of publications, including *The Jewish Advocate*, *The Harvard Review*, *Endicott Review*, and *Vallum*.

BEAR JACK GEBHARDT has been a freelance writer for many decades, with his seventh book (*The Potless Pot High—How to Get High, Clear and Spunky without Weed*) released this year. He has fiction, non-fiction, and poetry credits in a wide variety of national and international publications, including *The Columbia Journalism Review*, *The Christian Science Monitor*, *Jive*, *Fitness*, *Modern Maturity*, and *Hallmark*. His most recent stories have been sold to *Lake Country Journal* and *Hardboiled*.

JOSEPH GIORDANO was born in Brooklyn. He and his wife, Jane, lived in Greece, Brazil, Belgium and Netherlands. They now live in Texas with their little Shih Tzu, Sophia. Joe's stories appeared in more than thirty magazines including *Bartleby Snopes*, *The Foliate Oak*, and *The Summerset Review*.

MICHELLE HARTMAN's first book of poetry, *Disenchanted and Disgruntled*, from Lamar University Press, is available online. Her work can also be found in *Crannog*, *Poetry Quarterly*, and *The Pedestal Magazine*, as well as in numerous anthologies. A Pushcart nominee, her work has also appeared overseas in Ireland, Germany, Australia, Canada, and Nepal. She is also the editor of the award-winning journal *Red River Review*.

WILLIAM OGDEN HAYNES is a poet and author of short fiction from Alabama who was born in Michigan and grew up a military brat. His first book of poetry, *Points of Interest*, appeared in 2012, and a second collection of poetry and short stories, *Uncommon Pursuits*, was published in 2013. He has also published over seventy poems and short stories in literary journals, and his work has been anthologized multiple times.

JULEIGH HOWARD-HOBSON has simultaneously written literary fiction, formalist poetry, and genre work, along with non-fiction essays and articles, purposely blunting the modern "brandable" concept of artistic obligation to any single form or movement. Named a Million Writers Award "Notable Story" writer, her work has been nominated for both the Pushcart Prize and Best of the Net, and has appeared in print and online venues in England, Scotland, USA, Canada, Australia, Germany, Norway, and Africa, including *The Liar's League, The First Line, The Lyric, The Best of the Barefoot Muse* (Barefoot Pub), *Chick Ink: 40 Stories of Tattoos and The Women Who Wear Them* (Adams Media), and *Caduceus: The Poets at Art Place* Vol 8 (Yale University).

DOUG HOLDER is the founder of the Ibbetson Street Press. He teachings writing at Endicott College in Beverly, Mass and Bunker Hill Community College in Boston.

ANN HOWELLS's poetry has recently appeared in *Calyx, Crannog* (Ire), and *Free State Review*. She serves on the board of Dallas Poets Community, a 501-c-3 non-profit, and has edited its journal, *Illya's Honey*, since 1999. Her chapbook, *Black Crow in Flight*, was published by Main Street Rag Publishing (2007). Another chapbook, *The Rosebud Diaries*, was published in limited edition by Willet Press (2012). She has been nominated twice for both the Pushcart and Best of the Net.

JENNIFER JEAN's most recent book of poetry is *The Fool* (Big Table Publishing); she's also the author of *The Archivist* and *In the War*; as well, she's released *Fishwife Tales*, a collaborative CD. Her poetry, essays, and book reviews have been published in numerous journals, including: *Drunken Boat, Poetica, Tidal Basin Review,* and *The Mom Egg Review*. Jennifer blogs for Amirah, a non-profit advocating for sex-trafficking survivors. She teaches writing and literature at Salem State University.

TED JEAN is a carpenter who writes, paints, and plays tennis with lovely Lai Mei. His work appears in *Beloit Poetry Journal*, *DIAGRAM*, *Juked*, *Pear Noir*, *Gargoyle*, *Magma* (UK), and dozens of other publications.

LAWRENCE KESSENICH won the 2010 Strokestown International Poetry Prize. His poetry has been published in *Sewanee Review*, *Atlanta Review*, *Poetry Ireland Review*, and many other magazines. His chapbook *Strange News* was published by Pudding House Publications in 2008. In 2012, his poem "Underground Jesus" was nominated for a Pushcart Prize. *Before Whose Glory*, Kessenich's first full-length book, was published by FutureCycle Press in March 2013. Kessenich has had three short plays produced and has also published essays—one of which was featured on NPR's *This I Believe* in 2010 and appears in the anthology *This I Believe: On Love*.

LESLEY KIMBALL won an award for the project *Borderlands* in the Portsmouth Poet Laureate Program's "Voice and Vision" public art project. The interactive poetry sculpture is permanently installed at the Portsmouth Public Library. Her poem "Devotional" was featured by the NH Center for the Book and she was featured in the NH Poet Laureate's Poet Showcase in 2009 and 2013. Her poems have appeared in *Omphalos*, *The Pedestal Magazine*, and *Ink-Filled Page*, and the anthologies *The Other Side of Sorrow* and the 2010 *Poets' Guide to NH*. Lesley lives and writes in Portsmouth NH.

SVETLANA KORTCHIK's short stories have appeared or are about to appear in *Spark: A Creative Anthology*, *Forging Freedom*, *Alt Hist*, *94 Creations*, *Magination*, *Harvest Time* (Inwood Indiana Press anthology), *Gold Dust*, *Nazar Look*, *Bengal Lights*, *Eclectic Eel*, and *Alfie Dog*. She was the winner of the Historical Novel Society Autumn 2012 Short Fiction competition, and one of her stories has also been on the Commendations List of the Aesthetica Creative Works Competition 2010.

CHARLES LEGGETT is a professional actor based in Seattle, WA. His publications include *The Lyric* and *Measure: A Review Of Formal Poetry*. He has a tanka forthcoming in *Bottle Rockets*, and his long poem, "Premature Tombeau for John Ashbery," is an e-chapbook in the Barnwood Press "Great Find" series. His play, *The River's Invitation*, was featured at Seattle's Theatre Off Jackson as part of its inaugural Solo Performance Festival, "SPF 1: No Protection!" in March 2007. Charles also spent three years as lyricist/frontman for the Seattle blues band Uncle Ed's Molasses Jam, and currently writes, co-arranges, and performs blues tunes for the Sandbox Radio Orchestra.

NEIL MATHISON is an essayist and short-story writer who has been a naval officer, a nuclear engineer, an expatriate businessman living in Hong Kong, a corporate vice-president, and a stay-at-home-dad. His work has appeared in *The Ontario Review, Georgia Review, Southern Humanities Review, North American Review, North Dakota Quarterly, AGNI, Under the Sun, -divide-, Bellowing Ark, Pangolin Papers, Blue Mesa Review, Northwind, Blue Lyra Review*, and elsewhere. Forthcoming are short stories in *The Write Room* and *The Circus Book* and essays in *Moon City Review* and *Cold Mountain Review*. He lives and write in Seattle. His essay, "Volcano: an A to Z" was recognized as a "notable essay" in *Best American Essays 2010*. His essay "Redwoods" is a 2012 Pushcart nominee. Learn more at http://www.neilmathison.net/.

MARK J. MITCHELL studied writing at UC Santa Cruz under Raymond Carver, George Hitchcock, and Barbara Hull. His work has appeared in various periodicals over the last thirty five years, as well as the anthologies *Good Poems, American Places, Hunger Enough*, and *Line Drives*. His chapbook, *Three Visitors*, has recently been published by Negative Capability Press. *Artifacts and Relics*, another chapbook, is forthcoming from Folded Word, and his novel, *Knight Prisoner*, will be published in the coming months. He lives in San Francisco with his wife, the documentarian and filmmaker Joan Juster.

IVAN DE MONBRISON is a contemporary artist and writer from Paris, France. His works have been published and shown globally. His art can be seen on his website : http://artmajeur.com/blackowl/.

ROLAND PEASE is the poetry and fiction editor at Steerforth Press. He founded and edited Zoland Books for fifteen years. He edits *Zoland Poetry*, and his work has been published in *The Paris Review*, *The Boston Globe*, and *The New York Times*.

RICHARD KING PERKINS II is a state-sponsored advocate for residents in long-term care facilities. He has a wife, Vickie, and a daughter, Sage. His work has appeared in hundreds of publications. He has poems forthcoming in *The William and Mary Review*, *Bluestem*, and *Two Thirds North*.

JENNY ROSSI is an emerging writer from Vermont with work at *Strange Horizons*, a notable speculative fiction venue, and a chapbook out on Deadly Chaps Press titled *Riches for One, Poverty for Two*.

LUKE SALISBURY is the author of *The Answer is Baseball* and *The Cleveland Indian*. He teaches at Bunker Hill Community College and lives in Chelsea, MA.

FRANK SCOZZARI's fiction has previously appeared in various literary magazines, including *The Kenyon Review*, *South Dakota Review*, *The Nassau Review*, *Roanoke Review*, *Pacific Review*, *Reed Magazine*, *Folio*, *Ellipsis Magazine*, *Eureka Literary Magazine*, *The MacGuffin*, *Foliate Oak Literary Journal*, *Hawai'i Pacific Review*, *Chrysalis Reader*, and many others. His writing awards include winning the National Writer's Association Short Story Contest and three publisher nominations for the Pushcart Prize of Short Stories.

LOGAN SEIDL lives in Sparks, NV and is currently attending Truckee Meadows Community College. He is an aspiring writer whose articles, poetry, and fiction have been published or are forthcoming in *The Meadow*, *Crack the Spine*, *The Echo*, and *Writing Raw*. Logan is a prose board member for TMCC's literary and arts journal *The Meadow*. He would like to thank his wife Judi "Lady Fish" Seidl for her support and dedication to his craft. To learn more about Logan, visit http://loganseidl.com/.

ZVI A. SESLING has published poetry in numerous magazines both in print and online in the United States, Great Britain, New Zealand, Canada, and Israel. Among the publications are: *Ibbetson Street*, *Midstream*, *Poetica*, *Voices Israel*, *Saranac Review*, *New Delta Review*, *Plainsong*, *Asphodel*, *Istanbul Literary Review*, *The Chaffin Journal*, *Ship of Fools*, and *Main Street Rag*. He was awarded Third Place (2004) and First Prize (2007) in the Reuben Rose International Poetry Competition and was a finalist in the 2009 Cervena Barva Press Chapbook Contest. In 2008 he was selected to read his poetry at New England/Pen "Discovery" by Boston Poet Laureate Sam Cornish. He was a featured reader in the 2010 Jewish Poetry Festival in Brookline, MA. He is a regular reviewer for the Boston Small Press and Poetry Scene and he edits the *Muddy River Poetry Review* and publishes *Muddy River Books*. He is author of *King of the Jungle* (Ibbetson St., 2010), which has been nominated for the Massachusetts Book Award, and a chapbook *Across Stones of Bad Dream* (Cervena Barva, 2011) and a second full length poetry book, *Fire Tongue*, to be published by Cervena Barva Press.

A dynamic professional photographer, NARENDRA SHARMA captures the essence of an event with cherished details that make each event unique. His images display style and eye for composition and are worth saving for future memories. Narendra has earned various awards with NHPPA (New Hampshire Professional Photographer association). He has been recognized and appreciated by various organizations for his good work.

RUTH MARGOLIN SILIN has been writing for several years, more so in retirement. Living on a college campus retirement community offers her opportunities for continuing education, and having successful poets as her neighbors and fellow workshop participants is an added bonus. Prior to retirement she was Director of Development at a pediatric hospital in Brighton, MA. She now helps out in her daughter's boutique, where she writes rough drafts of poems in between customers. Boston is her home town; she went through the Boston schools and graduated from Northeastern U. Her poems have appeared in *Ibbetson Street*, *HazMat Review*, and *Hidden Oak*, and one is forthcoming in *Main Street Rag*.

HELEN SILVERSTEIN writes across genres and has published in journals as diverse as *Specs*, *OBIT*, and *Big Pulp*. She edits fiction and nonfiction for *Southern Women's Review*.

WENDELL SMITH is a physician who thinks "cures are facts, healing poetic" and is aware of the sprung rhetorical symmetry of that assertion. He knew Ramon Guthrie and Alexander Laing because of the Thursday Poets.

KATHLEEN SPIVACK's memoir, *With Robert Lowell and His Circle: Plath, Sexton, Rich, Bishop, Kunitz and Others*, was recently published by the University Press of New England. She is the author of seven previous books of prose and poetry (Doubleday, Graywolf etc.) *A History of Yearning* (2010), the Sow's Ear Poetry Chapbook winner, was awarded the London Book Festival First Prize. She has held Fulbright, Radcliffe Institute, NEA, and other fellowships. Her new novel, *Unspeakable Things*, is forthcoming from Knopf.

JOANNA M. WESTON is married and has two cats, multiple spiders, a herd of deer, and two derelict hen-houses. Her middle-reader, *Those Blue Shoes*, was published by Clarity House Press, and her book of poetry, *A Summer Father*, was published by Frontenac House of Calgary. For more about her eBook, *The Willow Tree Girl*, see her blog: http://www.1960willowtree.wordpress.com/.

CONSTELLATIONS
VOLUME 4

DISTRACTIONS

FALL 2014

In addition to publishing general unthemed content, in Volume 4 we hope to feature a selection of material exploring the theme of **Distractions**.

If you'd like to submit your poetry, fiction, or black and white art or photography for consideration, our reading period will run from February 15th through July 15th of 2014. For complete and updated submission guidelines or to submit online, please visit www.constellations-lit.com.

Made in the USA
Charleston, SC
22 December 2013